SECRET PROPHECY OF FATIMA REVEALED— NEW AGE VISIONS OF THE VIRGIN MARY

by Timothy Green Beckley & Art Crockett

Cover designed by Barbara Lynn

Graphics by Cosmic Computerland Systems

INNER LIGHT PUBLICATIONS
ISBN 0-938294-13-X

Introduction:
Fatima Decoded

While this book dramatically documents the apparition at Fatima, and reveals the "secret" of the lady's third prophecy, I hope to use these pages as a stepping stone to prove that visions of the "Virgin Mary," the "Blessed Mother" or "Our Lady in White" are not isolated phenomena, but that such visions are actually growing in intensity as we approach the beginning of a New Age which is drawing down new, feminine, energies onto the planet. For with rapidly spreading talk of "saving the planet," it is only natural that the symbol "Mother of us all" appears in physical form to make her love and blessings felt by everyone.

Even if only on a subconscious level, there are signs all around us that such illuminated manifestations have had an impact on our culture. Who would ever think that the Beatles, for instance, would write a song in which Paul McCartney croons, *"When I find myself in times of trouble Mother Mary comes to me speaking words of wisdom, Let it Be, Let it Be."*

Truly, there can be little doubt in anyone's mind upon reading through the maze of available literature that something utterly profound happened at Fatima, Portugal, on October 13th, 1917, when thousands gathered for a miracle which had been promised by three local children. Peering up into the dark, cloud filled sky, the throng witnessed a spectacle that has deservedly gone down in history as one of the greatest spiritual events of this—or any other—century.

In that rain soaked field, tens of thousands standing about literally fell to their knees as they observed the sun—or what they perceived to be the sun—spin from its lofty orbit and come so close to the ground that beams of colored light could be seen radiating in all directions upon the earth. Some described the "Miracle of the Falling Sun" as a whirling wheel of fire that scorched the soil, drying up the muddy land within moments of its descention from the heavens. Others spoke of nearly being blinded by the brilliant shafts that seemed to fly off the surface of the sun right into their eyes and onto their bodies. Not a person—believer or skeptic—went away feeling that he or she had not been touched by something super-natural. Indeed, many of this heavily atheistic crowd were converted overnight to the ways of the church from their pre-viously strong communistic viewpoint on God and creation.

Today, as we approach the end of an age, millions continue to flock yearly to Fatima to be cured of all manner of physical, mental and emotional ailments. Many say that the air around Fatima still seems to be filled with unknown energies which can, of its own volition, bless and heal saint and sinner alike.

That three, wide-eyed, innocent children could stir up such passions of faith, hope and charity that have lasted for decades, is just about proof enough that their vision of a lady engulfed in a blinding light was not a group fantasy or a mass hallucination, but was a subjective reality based on what their individual senses told them was really happening.

The reader, in fact, does not have to go about the task of cracking open dusty old books to realize fully the spectrum of such apparitions in our modern-day world. It has become com-mon knowledge that visions of the Virgin Mary have become fairly widespread. A person has only to pick up one of the many supermarket tabloids to learn about sightings every-where from Omaha to Chicago, from Paris to Havana.

On the other hand, if one wishes to skirt over such seem-ingly sensationalistic accounts as an apparition of Mary appearing on the side of a refrigerator, one merely has to step into any Catholic bookstore and find the section devoted to such sacred matters. Here the testimonials of the pious are quite plain, taking up volume after volume. Interestingly enough, it appears that visions of the Virgin Mary have increased many-fold since Fatima, and most assuredly so since the end of World War II and the beginning of the nuclear age.

The Marian or Madonna phenomena—as it is most often referred to—has recently attracted its share of scholarly researchers, many of whom are not associated with any particular denomination, nor are they necessarily even religiously oriented.

The Patterns

Instead, these investigators pour through tons of testimonials searching for possible clues and patterns that will lend additional credibility to the scores of case histories now recorded. Many of these patterns are noted throughout the pages of this book which, hopefully, will awaken scores to the fact that something of tremendous importance is taking place which needs to be re-evaluated.

One noteworthy pattern is that often, at the time of such materializations, the Lady will entrust to some worthy soul prophecies of forthcoming events. Sometimes the predictions are limited in scope and are of a personal nature of benefit or interest to just the immediate witness (such as that they will be turning to the priesthood or will be joining a convent). Other times they may be in the form of dire warnings that someone's life is in danger. Or the Lady can bring with her news pertaining to the nearest town or community, perhaps communicating the sad news of a forthcoming flood, or bridge disaster, or train wreck, that is certain to cause many deaths and bring great sorrow in its wake.

On other occasions, she may appear before some tragic world event such as a devastating earthquake or the outbreak of war. She may be seen by only one or two individuals, or by a small group, or perhaps by hundreds (or even thousands) gathered in a particular locality awaiting her arrival. Frequently, the Lady will appear over and over at one spot before vanishing never to be seen again. Other times the apparition is a "one shot" deal, and comes totally unannounced and unexpected. As proof, some of the gathered flock may be healed. Some may develop strange powers such as levitation or a sixth sense. Others may go into a trance state and "speak" directly with her. Those with cameras at their side have caught some truly amazing phenomena on film. Some have photographed glowing bursts that look remarkably like a lady engulfed in white light. Others pick up enigmatic strobes, flashes, and maybe even a form dressed in a robe.

Since they say a photo is worth a thousand words, we have decided to include as many of these unexplainable pictures in our possession as is possible without cutting down on the text.

Unearthly Explanations

Noted author John A. Keel, who has made a study of puzzling phenomena most of his life, has gone on record as stating that the most impressive UFO sighting of all time was the apparition of the falling sun associated with the vision of the Virgin Mary in Fatima. "I have seen photographs of the phenomena which were published at the time and the sun actually looks very much like a spinning disc."

Michael Grosso, a Ph.D. who teaches and lectures in New York, goes a step further when he proclaims, "To me, the events at Fatima look as if they were engineered by an intelligence of unknown origin." To back up his case that UFOs figure very deeply in this miracle, Grosso points that many of the "witnesses at Fatima reported observing thunderlike sounds, sounds of 'rockets,' sudden winds, drops in temperature, dimming of the sun and atmosphere, light effects that tinted trees, faces and stones, and 'falling flowers,' an effect similar to the 'angel hair' described in association with some

UFO sightings." He also notes that mysterious "flashes and balls of light were seen and the children involved reported being penetrated by a light ray, another common feature in UFO reports." Similarly, during the summer of 1917 (leading up to the sun's dancing) the children experienced, according to Grosso, "voicelike buzzings, smokelike forms, and Lucia was heard saying the lady disappeared through a *door* in the sky."

During my own tenure as a reporter interviewing witnesses of various unexplained phenomena, often times I couldn't be absolutely certain if I was being told about a close encounter with an extraterrestrial, or being offered another possible explanation for an apparition of the Virgin Mary. Actually, the vision seems to be saying it doesn't matter what you believe *as long* as you believe.

For example, there was the account related by rock guitarist-singer-songwriter Billy Squier who was a teenager at the time of his experience. "I was living in Wellesley, Massachusetts, and one summer afternoon a group of three or four of us guys were out on the golf course, on the 10th hole, about to tee off, when we all noticed a peculiar glow off in the woods."

Initially, Squier thought it might be the sun setting, but he soon realized it was too early in the day. Suddenly, a strange figure appeared out of nowhere in the midst of a glow, and they all saw it at once. "I had to blink twice to make sure I wasn't imagining things," Billy revealed. "The figure was that of a woman, and I would say she looked something like a madonna—you know, like a holy statue." The talented musician insists that the figure remained stationary for close to half a minute, and then disappeared in front of everyone's eyes as if entering another dimension. He felt it was both "incredible" and "baffling," and he's happy there were others present to verify what he'd seen.

In the pages to follow, we allow the witnesses and those involved first hand in such phenomena to speak for themselves, with as little editorial "tinkering" as possible that would change their words and ultimately their beliefs. Our own inter-pretations are clearly stated and are based on our own back-grounds and personal findings. Much of the material may seem overly "Catholic" in orientation, which is possibly the case since the Church has—rightfully—adopted Fatima into its accredited teachings (though they have been slow to accept similar Marian apparitions), while other Christian denomina-tions have by-passed such visions totally.

But most important, by no means are all the witnesses Catholic—for it seems apparent that the Marian phenomenon attaches itself to people of all ages from all walks of life—as the remainder of this book, I believe, will most certainly clarify!

Pope John Paul II and Our Lady of Fatima

The coincidence was startling. Just after 5:00 p.m. on May 13, 1981, Pope John Paul was shot while riding in a white jeep through St. Peter's Square. It was just after 5:00 p.m. on May 13, 1917, that three devout little children tending sheep in a field near Lisbon, saw the Virgin Mary.

The Pope was still in the hospital recovering from the Turkish radical's bullet when he decided to go to the Basilica of Our Lady of Fatima to give thanks to Mary for pulling him through.

Mehmet Ali Agca, the Turk who shot the Pope, would have a counterpart in a Spanish priest named Juan Fernandez y Krohn, 32. When Pope John Paul finally made his pilgrimage to Fatima on May 12, 1982, Fernandez lunged at him with a 16-inch bayonet. The attacker was only three feet from the Pope when he was stopped. Pope John Paul turned to bless his would-be killer even as Fernandez screamed, "Down with the Pope! Down with Vatican Two!"

Pope John Paul had little to say about Fernandez but the incident did not deter him in any way. He carried his lighted candle to the shrine and said a special Mass before 500,000 pilgrims gathered on the esplanade facing the shrine. He spoke to the people about the "menace of evil" he saw spreading throughout the world. He called on the Madonna for deliverance "from famine and war...from sin against the life of man from its very beginning...from hatred...from every kind of injustice in the life of society."

The Pope's Devotion to Mary

Pope John Paul is convinced that his remarkable recovery from his bullet wounds, was the result of the intervention of the Blessed Virgin. In December 1982 he told an audience, "I have seen the extraordinary maternal protection that showed itself to be more powerful than the homicidal bullets."

The Pope's devotion to Mary is unabashed and certainly no secret. His feelings for Mary have been fervent even when he was Karol Wojtyla, Bishop of Krakow, Poland. At that time he had an "M" for Mary embroidered on his robes. Now that he is Pope, his blue-and-white shield bears the same letter, and his personal motto is "Totus tuus sum Maria," which is Latin for "Mary, I am all yours." He has also visited most of the Marian shrines in the world.

The True Age of Mary

The Middle Ages is generally considered the golden age of the cult of Mary. However, there are many theologians, historians and sociologists who don't agree. One of them is Rev. James LeBar, spiritual advisor of the Blue Army, an international Catholic lay organization with its American headquarters at Our Lady of Fatima shrine in Washington, New Jersey. He says: "We have wars, threats of war, cults, drugs and a thousand other problems. People are looking frantically for help, and in Mary, they find it."

Rev. LeBar is convinced that the 20th century is the age of Mary.

Another who feels the same way is Ann Matter of the University of Pennsylvania. She is a specialist in the history of Christianity, and says: "This is the most active age of devotion to the Virgin. Not the 12th century, not the 9th, but right now.

"The interest has been building for the past 150 years, with more and more reports of visions of Mary in more and more places."

The fact is that attendance is 50 percent higher from last year at the shrine in Washington, New Jersey. Other shrines dedicated to the Madonna also report heavy increases in attendance. Also on the increase are offerings in Mary's name. Several shrines endorsed by the Vatican are Fatima, Lourdes and Knock, Ireland. Each year tens of thousands of pilgrims visit those shrines and pray to Mary for help with physical ailments, deformities and personal problems.

And they agree with the Pope when he said at Fatima: "It is always with emotion that I could have done or will ever do in the service of the holy church."

Mary's Place in Heaven and on Earth

Mary is exalted above all of the saints, angels and humans. She is venerated, but not worshiped. Only God may be worshiped. In the years of upheaval following the worldwide Vatican II assembly, traditionalists felt that Mary's role was downplayed. There were factions which felt that Mary would become as important as Jesus Christ. Nevertheless, Pope Paul in 1974 issued a 30,000-word document on Mary which proclaimed her as a "new woman" who was active in the early church and one who always sided with the weak against the powerful. What the document did was to notify the male-dominated church that Mary was a force to be reckoned with.

Fatima's Third Prophecy—1960

The year 1960 was eventful in one way, yet in another, it wasn't. Catholics and non-Catholics flooded Catholic information centers with questions about Fatima's third prophecy. What the curious asked was: "Was the Fatima prophecy going to be opened?" and, "When would it be revealed?" During the early part of 1960, St. Patrick's Cathedral in New York City received thousands of calls, with most of the callers asking those two questions.

The prophecy was opened, all right. The contents were sent to Rome, but the prophecy was not revealed. It may be revealed. It may be revealed at some time, and then again it may never be revealed. The Pope is the only one who can decide the issue.

Shortly after it was opened, there was great speculation about the prophecy everywhere. One rumor had it that the Pope read the prophecy in the presence of a bishop and both were so shocked that neither was able to speak.

Another rumor said that the prophecy warned of the church's destruction because the Western world had refused to heed the admonitions concerning penance and devotion. Still another rumor was that the Catholic Church was ordered to distribute its wealth to the poor no matter what their denomination.

There are factions which deny that there was a third

11

prophecy, that the contents were merely a recommendation or suggestion by Sister Lucy, the survivor of the trio who reported their visions, that if the West did not return to the church the Russians would chastise it.

In his book, *The Door to the Future,* Jess Stearn tells us that there was a spirit of de-emphasis concerning the third prophecy. The author says that in 1939 the third prophecy was placed in an unsealed package and turned over to Sister Lucy's bishop in Portugal for safekeeping until it was to be opened in 1960.

A church dignitary told Stearn, "Sister Lucy had been ill, and the bishop thought it might be a good idea to take down any further recollections she might have of the visions. There was nothing significant about his request or her compliance, or even the date. The whole thing was exaggerated out of all relation to reality."

If that were the case, Stearn reasoned, then why not reveal it and squelch all the rumors?

The dignitary replied: "Because it is time to discourage those who have tried to make a cult out of the prophecies instead of the worship."

What Others Say

Significant or not, there was a message. Part of its importance lies in the fact that it came from a nun who had the rare opportunity of seeing the Holy Mother in a vision.

Monsignor Harold Colgan, spiritual founder of the Blue Army (mentioned earlier), was in Portugal when the prophecy was opened in 1960. He said that the Bishop of Leiria sent it on to the Pope. The monsignor said that there was a lot of speculation about it, "but there is nothing unusual about the contents of the envelope not being revealed. It could be revealed tomorrow, in five years, two hundred, or never. The church itself is eternal, and time itself is unimportant."

Another Catholic dignitary in Portugal opined that the message had something to do with Russia, but that it was being kept a secret so that its contents would not add to world tensions.

Fatima Prophecy Still a Mystery?

The church said nothing officially about the Fatima prophecy in 1960. Then 1961 was almost over and there still was no long-awaited revelation. Finally, on October 6, 1961, the National Catholic Welfare Council published a disclaimer of the prophecy. The date was significant. October 6 was the eve of the worldwide pilgrimage to Fatima.

The disclaimer was written by Monsignor J.D. Conway. He wrote, in part: "I do not reject the whole idea of the Fatima story, though I am not personally deeply impressed by it. I have no serious questions about the credibility of the apparitions—that was declared by the Bishop of Leiria after seven years of investigation and careful study by theologians. I am not opposed to the Fatima devotions—they involve penance, sacrifice, and rosary, and devotion to the Mother of Jesus. But I think it (Fatima) has been often misused for purposes bordering on superstition; as a threat to inspire fear, as a goal to hatred and superstition, as a club with which to fight political enemies—and I don't mean Russian."

The publication did nothing to enlighten us about what was in the third prophecy. The year passed, then other years, and the mystery remains.

Before The Furor

The deep interest in the third prophecy was not generated until the late fifties and early sixties. Before that, the church had accepted the visions of Lucy, Jacinta and Francisco, and had placed its emphasis on the actual words spoken by Mary to the children. In December 1948, for instance, a pamphlet was published by the Catholic Information Society of the New York Archdiocese. It quoted from the original message delivered by the Holy Mother:

"If my requests are heard, Russia will be converted and

13

there will be peace. Otherwise, great errors will be spread through the world, giving rise to wars and persecutions against the church; the good will suffer martyrdom, and the Holy Father will have to suffer much, different nations will be destroyed; but in the end my Immaculate Heart will triumph, and an era of peace will be conceded to humanity."

The pamphlet makes it clear that the visions, the messages and the reason for the holy visits were tied in with Russia's fates. the pamphlet said: "Twenty-seven days after Lenin and Trotsky arrived in Petrograd (now Leningrad), to take command of the Socialist Revolution in Russia, Our Blessed Lady, the Mother of God, appeared in a little cove outside the small town of Fatima, sixty miles north of Lisbon in Portugal. It was her sixth and last visit to warn the world of its folly and to offer a heavenly remedy."

The pamphlet mentioned nothing about the mystery of the third prophecy. That would come later. During the twenty-odd years since 1960, doubters have voiced their opinions and rumors have run rampant. There have been all sorts of learned statements about the mystery, but it might be best if we reviewed not only what happened in 1917, but take an inside look at the three young people involved.

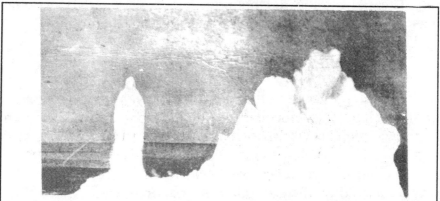

OMEN OF "OUR LADY OF THE FJORDS"—In 1905, on the anniversary of the discovery of Newfoundland by John Cabot, this spectacular iceberg showing the form of the Virgin Mary appeared on the narrows at the entrance to the harbor of the city of St. John. It was heralded as an omen of great change and though this land had been a tragic one, with many lives lost at sea and during storms, following this "Omen" a new era was born and Newfoundland eventually became part of Canada.

Photo: 13 July 1917 — The three little Shepherds near the Church

The Three Children

Jacinta Marto and Her Terrible Vision

Nearly everything we know about Lucia dos Santos and her cousins, Jacinta Marto and her brother Francisco, has come from the pen of Lucia dos Santos, who had the good sense to write a book about her life.

In her book, *Fatima,* Sister Lucy says of Jacinta: "Before the happenings of 1917, apart from the ties of relationship that united us, no other particular affection led me to prefer the companionship of Jacinta and Francisco to that of any other child. On the contrary, I sometimes found Jacinta's company quite disagreeable, on account of her oversensitive temperament. The slightest quarrel which arose among the children when at play was enough to send her pouting into a corner— 'tethering the donkey' as we used to say. Even the coaxing and caressing that children know so well how to give on such occasions, were still not enough to bring her back to play; she herself had to be allowed to choose the game, and her partner as well. Her heart, however, was well disposed. God had endowed her with a sweet and gentle character which made her at once lovable and attractive. I don't know why, but Jacinta and her brother Francisco had a special liking for me, and almost always came in search of me when they wanted to play. They did not enjoy the company of the other children, and they used to ask me to go with them to the well down at the bottom of the garden belonging to my parents."

According to Sister Lucy, Jacinta was an extremely devout little girl whose passion was to have Lucy tell her the story, again and again, of the sufferings of Our Lord. And at each telling, Jacinta would cry, saying: "Our poor dear Lord! I'll never sin again! I don't want Our Lord to suffer anymore!"

Some experts say that Jacinta's terrible vision, revealed just before her death, may be linked to the unrevealed prophecy which caused so much consternation in 1960. This vision or message, was investigated by a Jesuit Father named Fonseca.

According to Sister Lucy's telling of it, "Jacinta saw a terrible war, annihilated nations, many ruined houses, and streets filled with people crying with hunger and having nothing to eat. She saw the Holy Father before a table in a large house with his face in his hands, crying. Outside the house there were many people, some of whom cast stones at him while others reviled and cursed him.

"Afterwards she also saw many of the persecuted faithful, among whom were slain priests...until the blood of martyrs had placated the wrath of God. Many people will die in this war, the great majority of whom will go to hell. God will send great punishments into this world and Spain will be the first country to suffer."

Apparently, Jacinta referred to World War II, still far into the future. And, or course, Spain was the first nation to suffer, just as she predicted, when the Communists and the Axis Powers mixed it up in the prelude to World War II.

Francisco

Sister Lucy tells us: "The affection which bound me to Francisco was just one of kinship, and one which had its origin in the graces which heaven deigned to grant us.

"Apart from his features and his practice of virtue, Francisco did not seem at all to be Jacinta's brother. Unlike her, he was neither capricious nor vivacious. On the contrary, he was quiet and submissive by nature. He showed no love for dancing, as Jacinta did; he much preferred the flute while others danced.

"Francisco was a boy of few words. Whenever he prayed or offered sacrifices, he preferred to go apart and hide, even from Jacinta and myself. Quite often, we surprised him, hidden behind a wall or a clump of blackberry bushes, wither he had ingeniously slipped away to kneel and pray or think, as he said, 'of our Lord, Who is sad on account of so many sins.'

"Francisco was very fond of birds, and could not bear to see anyone robbing their nests. He always kept part of the bread he had for his lunch, breaking it into crumbs and spreading them out on top of the rocks, so that the birds could eat them.

"One day we met a little boy carrying in his hand a small bird that he had caught. Full of compassion, Francisco promised him two coins if only he would let the bird fly away. The boy readily agreed, but first he wanted to see the coins. Francisco ran all the way home from the Carreira pond, which lies a little distance below the Cova de Iria, to fetch the coins, and so let the little prisoner free. Then, as he watched it fly away, he clapped his hands for joy and said, 'Be careful! Don't let yourself be caught again.'

"Francisco was anything but fearful. He'd go anywhere in the dark alone at night, without the slightest hesitation. He played with lizards, and when he came across any snakes he got them to entwine themselves around a stick, and even poured sheep's milk into the holes in the rocks for them to drink. He went hunting for foxes' holes and rabbits' burrows, for genets, and other creatures of the wild."

Lucy Dos Santos

Lucy was 10 when she and her cousins were visited by the Holy Mother. Jacinta Marto was nine and Francisco was seven. Lucy was born on March 30, 1907. She was the youngest of seven children, six girls and a boy. In the beginning her companions were the boys and girls of Aljustrel, a hamlet belonging to the parish of Fatima. But as of 1917, Lucy's sole companions were her cousins, Jacinta and Francisco. This was the year of the apparitions. And it must be remembered that the Holy Mother spoke only to Lucy, and she alone was the only one of the three to remain on earth for a long period to fulfill her mission.

It was the Blessed Virgin who told Lucy to learn how to read, which she did as soon as the visions were over. She attended school and learned to read and write with an amazing speed.

At 14 she entered the College of Porto, where she excelled in her studies. From there she entered the novitiate and became a nun. Pilgrims on their way to the Fatima Shrine would stop at Coimbra to visit the Carmel and hear Lucy's voice in the nun's choir of the Discalced Carmelites.

Lucy's Silence

One church dignitary said of Sister Lucy: "She obviously saw the approaching war before it happened, because she referred it to the next pontificate, which would have been that of Pius XI, and though the war actually came in 1939, a few months after his death, many believe that Europe had been at war since 1936 when Hitler marched into the Rhineland. And, of course, the Spanish Civil War broke out in that pontificate, too."

But to this day there is some mystery as to why Lucy remained silent on the Holy Mother's statements about Russia. She said nothing about them until 1927, a full 10 years after the apparitions. One critic stated that at the time of the visions, Russia was hardly in a position to menace anyone. In the first place, she was an insignificant force in world affairs. She had been devastated by war, and she struggled with a five-year plan that kept her interested only in matters within her own borders.

Nevertheless, there is no reason now to mistrust the story of Fatima. The contents of the original message in 1917 and the prophecies are the same now as they were then. There were no changes.

The story was one of childish faith. A miracle had occurred. It restored the church's vigor in a nation in which the ruling powers were determined to eliminate Catholic worship. The miracle touched off a spiritual revolution without shedding a drop of blood. And that was a miracle in itself.

Pope Pius XII was intrigued by the story. So was Pope John XXIII. The Fatima story has interested Catholics and non-Catholics alike. The shrine of Fatima is one of the most popular in the world.

Upheaval in Portugal

At the time of the first vision, Portugal, known as the Land of Mary, was in a state of upheaval. The country that was known for its traditional devotion to the Immaculate Heart of Mary saw the monarchy overthrown by a revolutionary republican government. This new ruling power abolished the Catholic sacraments. It stated boastfully that in two generations the Catholic religion would be completely wiped out in Portugal.

That was easier said than done. In the hills of Fatima, where the peasants were extremely poor, the children of the poorest parish in Portugal clung to their rosaries. They and their parents would not be cowed by the government.

Three children in particular said their rosaries daily. They were Lucy, Jacinta and Francisco. Their job was to tend sheep in the pasture belonging to Lucy's father, Antonio. This pasture was on a high plateau that was called Cova de Iria. And it was on this plateau that the miracle occurred.

The Vision

The sky was cloudless on May 13, 1917. The three children were quiet. They were hard at work keeping the sheep bunched up and running after strays. Suddenly, there were two flashes of lightning. Now lightning in a cloudless sky was frightening, and it brought the children's attention up sharply. Perhaps it was meant to.

They stopped what they were doing and looked at the sky. Their attention was then focused on the leaves from an old oak tree. They saw a globe of light, and from it a sort of iridescent radiance. An aura appeared to develop in the center of the globe of light. Eventually, they could make out the figure of a woman. She appeared to be very young, perhaps 18.

Lucy, Jacinta and Francisco were frozen with fright. They stared wide-eyed. Then the woman said, "Do not be afraid. I will not harm you."

The apparition then disappeared almost as quickly as it appeared.

There was no identification. The vision did not say, "I am the Holy Mother." But she did ask the three children to return to the same spot on the 13th of every month until October. At that time, she said, she would reveal her identity. She urged the children to keep her presence a secret and to say their rosary everyday.

The three children did say their rosary everyday, but they did not keep the vision a secret. Lucy scolded them and cajoled them not to say a word, but the experience was so awe-inspiring that they could not contain themselves.

All three told their parents—and they were scolded for lying. Even the parish priest heard about their "lies" and made his displeasure known to them. Jacinta's mother was so angry with her daughter that she beat her. Still, Jacinta would not change her story, or admit that she lied.

The story spread through the hamlet and there were those who believed. In fact, when the three children went to the high plateau on June 13, some fifty to sixty villagers went with them.

Lucy was the acknowledged leader of the three. She faced the oak tree and said her rosary. Her face turned toward the east. Suddenly, she cried: "I've seen the lightning! The lady is coming!"

The villagers saw no lightning. They saw no vision. But they did see Lucy's face and watched it grow ecstatic. Lucy saw something in the foliage of the oak tree. So did Jacinta and Francisco. But the villagers saw nothing. They listened entranced to Lucy's excited questions, but did not hear the replies.

The Lady's Sad Message

The vision did not last long, but what the woman in the tree said startled all three children. She said that Jacinta and Francisco would soon go to heaven, but that Lucy would have to remain on earth to spread the message of the Immaculate Heart of Mary.

Lucy did not have any problem spreading the message. It spread by itself, and more quickly than the lighting on the high plateau. The village of Fatima held only a few hundred inhabitants, yet within days everyone in Portugal, or so it seemed, had heard about the strange vision. By the time July 13th rolled around, five thousand people traveled to Cova da Iria.

The Third Vision

During this visit, according to Lucy, the apparition said that World War I would end soon. Portugal was involved in the

22

struggle, and had been for a full year. The woman told the children: "But if people do not cease to offend God, not much time will elapse, and in the next pontificate, another and more terrible war will begin. When there is seen a night illumination by an unknown light, know that this is the great sign which God is giving that He is about to punish the world for its crimes by means of war, famine, persecutions of the church and of the Holy Father."

Lucy did not reveal the lady's next request for ten years. The request was to consecrate Russia to the Immaculate Heart. The hope was that Russia would be converted and peace would reign. The lady in the oak feared that Russia would become the scourge of God, as had Attila and his Huns. And she assured Lucy that in the end Christ would triumph.

The Government Steps In

After the third vision all of Portugal was aware of the miracle on the high plateau. And, of course, the government heard about it, too. Authorities sensed deep trouble for themselves. They were determined to wipe out the Catholic religion in Portugal, yet here were three children who were in effect starting a religious revolution.

The children had to be shown up as liars. That was the only way to stop this nonsense. So Lucy, Jacinta and Francisco were arrested and thrown into jail. The gesture was made not to punish the children but to keep them available to the authorities so that the youngsters could be bullied into making them retract their statements about the visions.

It didn't work. The children knew what they had seen and heard. It was foolish for anyone to think they would deny it.

As a last resort, the youngsters were shown a large vat of boiling oil. They were told that they would be thrown into it if they didn't confess that they had made up stories about the lady in the oak tree.

That didn't work. Not only would the children stick to their guns, but they also refused to divulge what the apparition told them. That, they said, was a secret.

Being locked up like criminals was bad enough, but the authorities had slyly jailed the youngsters at the very time the vision was supposed to make her next appearance—August 13th.

About fifteen thousand people showed up at Cova da Iria on that date, and it was then that they found out the blessed little children were in jail. They waited around on the high plateau, but saw only a white cloud and a flash of lightning. They did do a lot of talking, however, and they were outraged against the government for doing such a dastardly thing against two little girls and a boy.

So much unrest was stirred up, however, that the government decided that it would be expedient to release the children or suffer a real revolution. Lucy, Jacinta and Francisco went to the Cova after a few days, alone, and saw the vision. The fourth appointment was kept.

By this time all of Portugal was excited. The authorities were worried. They knew of no way to stop the mushrooming effect the little children were having on the nation. When September 13th rolled around, many people followed the youngsters to the high plateau.

All of them watched the children eagerly. When they looked toward the sky, the crowd did the same. Many witnesses reported seeing the mysterious white cloud in a cloudless sky. They said it rained, yet there were no clouds and the sun was shining. They also said they saw the bright globe in the small oak tree.

The Fifth Vision (September 13th, 1917)

Sister Lucy tells us in her book: "As the hour approached, I set out with Jacinta and Francisco, but owing to the crowds around us we could only advance with difficulty. There was no human respect whatsoever. Simple folk, and even ladies and gentlemen, struggled to break through the crowd that pressed around us. No sooner had they reached us then they threw themselves on their knees before us, begging us to place their petitions before Our Lady. Others that could not get close to us shouted from a distance.

"'For the love of God, ask Our Lady to cure my son who is a cripple.'

"Another man cried out: 'And to cure mine who is blind!...' To cure mine who is deaf!...To bring back my husband, my son, who has gone to war...To convert a sinner...To give me back my health because I have tuberculosis,' and so on.

"All the afflictions of poor humanity were assembled there. Some climbed up to the tops of trees and walls to see us go by, and shouted down to us. Saying yes to some, giving a hand to others and helping them up from the dusty ground, we managed to move forward, thanks to some gentlemen who went ahead and opened a passage for us through the multitude.

"Now, when I read in the New Testament about those enchanting scenes of Our Lord's passing through Palestine, I think of those which Our Lord allowed me to witness, while yet a child, on the poor roads and lanes from Aljustrel to Fatima and on to the Cova da Iria! I give thanks to God, offering Him the faith of our good Portuguese people, and I think: 'if these people so humbled themselves before three small and poor children, just because they were mercifully granted the grace to speak with the Mother of God, what would they not do if they saw Our Lord Himself in person before them?'

"Well, none of this was called for here. It was a distraction of my pen, leading me away where I did not mean to go. But, never mind! It's just another useless digression. I am not tearing it out, so as not to spoil the book.

"At last, we arrived at the Cova da Iria, and on reaching the holmoak we began to say the rosary with the people. Shortly afterwards, we saw the flash of light, and then Our Lady appeared in the holmoak.

"The Lady said: 'Continue to pray the rosary in order to obtain the end of the war. In October Our Lord will come, as well as Our Lady of Dolours and Our Lady of Carmel. Saint

Joseph will appear with the Child Jesus to bless the world. God is pleased with your sacrifices. He does not want you to sleep with the rope on, but only to wear it during the daytime.'

"I was told to ask you many things, the cure of some sick people, a deaf mute...

"'Yes, I will cure some, but not others. In October I will perform a miracle so that all may believe.'

"Then Our Lady began to rise as usual, and disappeared."

The Investigation

The Catholic Church always exhibits reserve on matters pertaining to miracles. It did so this time, as well. It would have been easy for the church to accept the miracle on blind faith if only to thumb its nose at the anti-Christs running the government. But it chose not to do so. One Catholic newspaper asked in a banner headline: "Real Apparition or Supposed Illusion?" And there were liberals who called the event the Farce at Cova da Iria.

The church in Lisbon decided to conduct an investigation. It asked the Reverend Doctor Manuel Nunes Formigao to see what was going on at Fatima.

After a preliminary probe, Rev. Formigao was startled by the similarity of the Fatima story with that of one that had taken place in La Salette, France. There, two shepherd children reported seeing Our Lady in a vision. The message was the same. Great calamities would visit France if the French people did not stop offending God.

Father Formigao questioned Lucy about the French story. Yes, she said, her mother told her about it, but it had not crossed her mind in some time. The priest then tried to get Lucy to reveal the secret told to her by Our Lady. Lucy refused. She said that if the crowd knew it there would be great sadness. Lucy added that she and Jacinta heard the secret, and that Francisco did not. He only saw the vision. She said that Our Lady would appear on October 13th and that she would perform a great miracle.

26

The investigator was stymied. He could not be sure how much of what Lucy said was fact, and how much was fiction. He resigned himself to wait until the appointed day before he made a judgment.

The Sixth Vision (October 13th, 1917)

Early that morning the roads leading to Fatima were clogged with people. Farmers, factory workers, rich and poor alike were anxious to see the miracle that Our Lady promised, and perhaps even to become cured of the ailments that afflicted them.

Sister Lucy tells us: "We left home quite early, expecting that we would be delayed along the way. Masses of people thronged the roads. The rain fell in torrents. My mother, her heart torn with uncertainty as to what was going to happen, and fearing it would be the last day of my life, wanted to accompany me.

"On the way, the scenes of the previous month, still more numerous and moving, were repeated. Not even the muddy roads could prevent these people from kneeling in the most humble and suppliant of attitudes."

Actually, many of the people traveled all night to reach the Cova da Iria by noon. And for some it was quite an ordeal because they carried their crippled and ailing children. Others could be seen hobbling along on crutches.

One reporter wrote later: "Nearly all, men and women have bare feet, the women carrying their footgear in bags on their heads, the men leaning on great staves and carefully grasping umbrellas also. One would say that they were all oblivious to what was going on about them, with a great lack of interest in the journey and in other travelers, as if lost in a dream, reciting their rosary in a sad rhythmic chant."

It was estimated that about 70,000 people made the pilgrimage to the Cova da Iria. All were soaked to the skin by the heavy rain. Toward noon the rain eased off into a drizzle, but by that time it didn't make any difference. Everyone was drenched.

Lucy, as usual, was in the lead. She stood before the hol-moak, or oak tree as we know it, and looked out at a sea of umbrellas. It had started to rain heavily again. Lucy shouted to the crowd, "Close your umbrellas!" The people obeyed and stood in the downpour unprotected.

It was noon. Nothing happened. The crowd became rest-less. A priest who was there as an observer decided to lead the children away. Everyone was wet. The children could catch colds, or worse.

Suddenly, Lucy cried: "She is coming! Kneel everybody!"

The little girl appeared to be looking at something, and lis-tening, but no one else could see what it was. Then Lucy asked the apparition: "What do you want of me?"

The Lady replied: "I want to tell you that a chapel will be built here in my honor. I am the Lady of the Rosary. Continue always to pray the rosary everyday. The war is going to end and the soldiers will return to their homes."

Lucy said: "I have many things to ask you: the cure of some sick persons, the conversion of sinners, and other things."

"Some, yes," the Lady said, "but not others. They must amend their lives and ask for forgiveness for their sins." According to Lucy, the Lady then looked very sad and said: "Do not offend the Lord our God anymore, because He is already so much offended."

The rain stopped abruptly. The clouds parted and the sun appeared in a bright, azure blue sky.

Lucy said: "Then, opening her hands, she made them reflect on the sun, and as she ascended, the reflection of her own light continued to be projected on the sun itself.

"Here, Your Excellency, is the reason why I cried out to the people to look at the sun. My aim was not to call their attention to the sun, because I was not even aware of their presence. I was moved to do so under the guidance of an inte-rior impulse.

"After Our Lady had disappeared into the immense distance of the firmament, we beheld St. Joseph with the Child Jesus and Our Lady robed in white with a blue mantle, beside the sun. St. Joseph and the Christ Jesus appeared to bless the world, for they traced the Sign of the Cross with their hands. When, a little later this apparition disappeared, I saw Our Lord and Our Lady; it seemed to me that it was Our Lady of Dolours. Our Lord appeared to bless the world in the same manner as St. Joseph had done. This apparition also vanished and I saw Our Lady once more, this time resembling Our Lady of Carmel."

It is not reported if any among the multitude saw these apparitions. What they did see, however, was equally as stunning. Many witnesses reported that the sun began to spin in much the same way that a firecracker wheel spins. It gave off fiery fingers of light that extended across the sky.

The earth itself seemed to change colors. First it was cast in a sort of red shadow, then orange, yellow, green, blue, indigo and violet. This phenomenon repeated itself three times. Then, quite suddenly, the sun began to plunge toward the earth. It shuddered as it came closer, shimmying violently. The crowd screamed. Some thought it was the end of the world. Thousands fell to their knees in abject terror. Others went prone, pleading with God to have mercy. Still others knelt, too frightened to speak, yet prayed silently as their eyes stared up at the approaching sun.

The weird display continued for 10 minutes. Finally, the sun halted in its devastating approach to earth and started to climb again to its normal position in the sky.

Editor de Almeida (Avelino) of a newspaper called *O Seculo,* wrote that day:

"Certainly beyond all cosmic laws, were the sudden tremblings and movements of the sun, dancing as it were, in typical language of the peasants, before the astonished multitude who gazed in awe. It remains for the competent to pronounce on the dance macabre of the sun, which today at Fatima has made hosannas burst from the breasts of the faithful and naturally has impressed—so witnesses worthy of belief assure me—even freethinkers and other persons not at all interested in religious matters. To this unbeliever it was a spectacle unique and incredible if one had not been a witness to it. One can see the immense crowd turn toward the sun, which reveals itself free of the clouds, and he hears the nearest spectators crying, 'Miracle, miracle.'"

It is interesting to note here that Avelino do Almeida was a skeptic and anti-clerical. He was a Freemason who had no belief in miracles. But on that day his resolve was shaken.

The Plight of the Three Children

There was no rest now for Lucy, Jacinta and Francisco. They were instant celebrities. Peaceful moments were out of the question now. Everywhere they went they were buttonholed and asked dozens of questions. Their pictures were taken again and again. They were asked to talk to groups. Reporters were forever hovering near. Every word they spoke was published.

Finally, the children began to withdraw into themselves. Jacinta, especially, was troubled. She had been a happy-go-lucky child; now she was sad. It was not the approach of her own death that worried her. Rather, it was the attention she received. She didn't want it. It smacked of adulation and she detested that.

Jacinta then began having visions of her own. They were quite prophetic. She was able to look 25 years into the future, where she saw horrible bombings along the roads of France and in Holland. She saw London and Frankfurt in ruins from the bombs.

Jacinta and Francisco knew they were gong to die soon because the Lady told them so. But they were not frightened. In fact, they looked forward to it.

Francisco's Holy Death

The end came for the little boy in April, 1919. He was sick

with influenza for nearly four months. Francisco was eleven years old.

Lucy wrote: "That night I said goodbye to him.

"'Goodbye, Francisco! If you get to heaven tonight, don't forget me when you get there, do you hear me?'

"'No,' he answered, 'I won't forget. Be sure of that.'

"Then, seizing my right hand, he held it tightly for a long time, looking at me with tears in his eyes.

"'Do you want anything more?' I asked him, with tears running down my cheeks, too.

"'No,' he answered in a low voice, quite overcome.

"As the scene was becoming so moving my aunt told me to leave the room.

"Goodbye then, Francisco! Till we meet in heaven, goodbye.

"Heaven was drawing near. He took his flight to heaven the following day in the arms of his Heavenly Mother. I could never describe how much I missed him. This grief was a thorn that pierced my heart for years to come. It is a memory of the past that echoes forever into eternity."

Jacinta's Holy Death

A few months after Francisco's death, Jacinta came down with the flu. Specialists recommended a difficult chest operation. The girl told Lucy that the Holy Mother had come to visit her and said that Jacinta would be transferred to a hospital in Lisbon and that she would die alone. She was right. Within six weeks Jacinta was moved to St. Stephens Hospital in Lisbon. She needed special care and surgery.

Jacinta reported that she had several visions during her sickness. The Virgin Mary came to see her a few times, and although everyone called her visions prophetic, Jacinta was merely repeating what the Holy Mother had told her.

For instance, Mother Gohindo, a Franciscan nun, who saw Jacinta daily, once remarked to the girl that she had heard of a wonderful sermon by a certain priest. Jacinta merely closed her eyes and said, "The padre is wicked. You will see." The nun recalled that a few months later the priest left the order under a cloud.

On another occasion a doctor who treated Jacinta asked the girl to pray for him before she went to heaven. Jacinta told him, "You and your daughter will be there before me." The doctor and his daughter died soon after, and Jacinta was still alive.

One afternoon she asked a nun to fetch a priest, that she wanted to make her First Communion and to confess her sins. That was done. The priest told Jacinta that he would bring the Holy Eucharist the first thing in the morning.

"That will be too late," Jacinta said. "I'm going to die tonight."

The priest talked to the doctors. They saw no danger. It would be all right, they said, if he brought the Holy Eucharist in the morning.

They were wrong. At 10:30 p.m., Jacinta worsened. Her nurse rushed away for a doctor, but when they returned, Jacinta was dead. She died alone, and in Lisbon, as she predicted. The date was February 20, 1920.

A Cardinal Impressed

Cardinal Patriarch Manuel Arejeira was impressed first by the astonishing phenomenon of the sun, and then by the children's deaths. He said: "The three little children confess that the Heavenly apparition had predicted that she would soon come after two of them to take them to heaven. During the illness that struck both, they insist that prayers and doctors will never cure them. One of them asserts that she will die alone, far from her family in a hospital, while the other runs from school to go to church, since it is not worth his while to learn how to read, and it all took place as they had predicted it."

Lucy Becomes a Nun

Shortly after the deaths of Jacinta and Francisco, Lucy

went to a convent school and took the name Sister Maria das Dores—Sister Mary of Sorrows. Her mission, as Lucy saw it, was to perpetuate the message of Fatima.

She clung to the secret about the chastisement of Russia and its eventual consecration to Christianity. In December 1925 she had another vision. Lucy was not in the convent of the Sisters of St. Dorothy in Tuy, Spain, which is across the border from Portugal. She saw the Holy Mother and the Christ Child. The Holy Mother told her: "My child, behold my heart surrounded with the thorns that ungrateful men place therein at every moment by their blasphemies and ingratitude. You at least try to console me."

One of Mary's Fatima prophecies was: "When you see a light lit up by an unknown light, know that this is the great sign God gives you that He is going to punish the world for its crimes by means of war..." On January 25, 1938, the sky throughout Europe glowed mysteriously and World War II started just 45 days later.

Additional Visions

After the visit, Lucy began in earnest to push for Our Lady's desire for the devotion to her Immaculate Heart. She talked to her confessors about it in 1926, 1927 and 1929. In 1940 she wrote to Pius XII. Lucy became a novice in 1926.

In 1927, Lucy had two visions of Jesus Christ. He confirmed the request of His mother concerning devotions. He gave Lucy permission to reveal certain things about the 1927 miracles, but told her that she must not reveal the last secret. Apparently, that was to be saved until 1960.

It was then, 1927, that Lucy revealed the threat from Russia. According to Lucy, she and her two cousins were told to look for a light in the sky. Of course, Jacinta and Francisco weren't here at that time, but Lucy was and she saw that warning about the beginning of World War II come as a light in the sky.

The Strange Light

The lights appeared all over Western Europe on January 25, 1938. There was a crimson glow, seemingly everywhere. One newspaper called it the Aurora Borealis and reported that hundreds of people panicked. Its copy said: "The lights were seen clearly in Italy, Spain and even Gibraltar...they spread fear in parts of Portugal, while thousands of Britons were brought running into the streets in wonderment."

Sister Lucy made no mention of the lights until 1941, when she wrote to the Bishop of Leiria: "Your Excellency is not unaware that some years ago God manifested that sign which the astronomers choose to designate by the Aurora Borealis. If they look well into it, they will see that it was not and could not be, in the form in which it appeared, such an aurora. But be that as it may, God was pleased in this way to make me understand that His justice was ready to let fall the blow of the guilty nations, and in this way to begin to ask with insistence for the reparatory communion of the first Saturdays and the consecration of Russia."

In 1946 Lucy told William Thomas Walsh, an American Catholic scholar: "What our Lady wants is that the Pope and all the bishops in the world shall consecrate Russia to her Immaculate Heart on one special date. If it is not done, the errors of Russia will spread through every country in the world."

Walsh asked her, "Does this mean, in your opinion, that every country without exception will be overcome by communism?"

Lucy answered: "Yes."

Mary's Plea Concerning Russia

On June 13th, 1929, Lucy had a vision of the Most Holy Trinity, with Our Lady showing her Heart, in the chapel of her convent at Tuy, Spain.

Lucy's notes on this vision are as follows:

"Rev. Fr. Jose Bernardo Goncalves sometimes came to our chapel to hear confessions. I went to confession to him and as I felt at ease with him, I continued to do so for the three years that he remained here as Assistant to the Fr. Provincial.

"It was at this time that Our Lady informed me that the moment had come in which she wished me to make known to the Holy Church her desire for the consecration of Russia, and her promise to convert it. The communication was as follows:

"13-6-29. I had sought and obtained permission from my superiors and confessor to make a Holy Hour from eleven o'clock until midnight, every Thursday to Friday night. Being alone one night, I knelt near the altar rails in the middle of the chapel and, prostrate, I prayed the prayers of the Angel. Feeling tired, I then stood up and continued to say the prayers with arms in the form of a cross. The only light was that of the sanctuary light, and above the altar appeared a cross of light, reaching to the ceiling. In a brighter light on the upper part of the cross could be seen the face of a man and his body as far as the waist; upon his breast was a dove of light; nailed to the cross was the body of another man. A little below the waist I could see a chalice and a large host suspended in air, on which drops of blood were falling from the face of Jesus crucified and from the wound in His side. These drops ran down on the host and fell into the chalice. Beneath the right arm of the cross was Our Lady and in her hand was her Immaculate Heart. (It was Our Lady of Fatima, with her Immaculate Heart in her left hand, without sword or roses, but with a crown of thorns and flames). Under the left arm of the cross, large letters, as if of crystal clear water which ran down upon the altar, formed these words:

"Grace and Mercy."

"I understand that it was the mystery of the Most Holy Trinity which was shown to me, and I received lights about this mystery which I am not permitted to reveal.

"Our Lady then said to me: 'The moment has come in which God asks the Holy Father, in union with all the bishops of the world, to make the consecration of Russia to my Immaculate Heart, promising to save it by this means. There are so many souls whom the Justice of God condemns for sins committed against me, that I have come to ask reparation: sacrifice yourself for this intention and pray.'

"I gave an account of this to the confessor, who ordered me to write down what Our Lady wanted done.

"Later, in an intimate communication, Our Lord complained to me, saying:

"They did not wish to heed my request. Like the King of France, they will repent and do it, but it will be late. Russia will have already spread her errors throughout the world, provoking wars, and persecutions of the Church: the Holy Father will have much to suffer."

What Holy Father?

Undoubtedly, Our Lord was talking about Pope John Paul II, who has already suffered a serious bullet wound and another assassination attempt. He has seen his country (Poland) stripped of every vestige of freedom. During his papacy he has seen Russia invade Afghanistan. He has seen Iran and Iraq in mortal conflict. He has witnessed the conflict between Great Britain and Argentina. He suffers with the unrest of South and Central America, where people are being murdered in their homes.

There can be little doubt that Our Lord referred to our present Holy Father, who is suffering and will suffer a great deal more before death claims him.

Two French policemen photographed a UFO in the sky—when the photo was developed the image of a cross could be seen quite plainly.

Age of Mary

As previously stated, we are truly in the Marian Age at this time. We have had more visions of the Holy Mother and other holy figures in the past twenty to thirty years than at any other period in history. The Virgin has materialized not only in places one might expect her to appear, but she has also manifested herself in alien quarters, among countries and religious groups who are not at all sympathetic with the Christian cause. The Virgin Mary, too, most often appears to children, just as she did in Fatima, with Sister Lucy, Jacinta and Francisco.

In fact, when you examine the number of times that Mary has appeared on earth, and when you understand that her visions were seen first by children, you begin to realize that there are scores of "Fatimas" throughout the world. Not so dramatic perhaps as the visions which appeared in Portugal, but nevertheless true visions, most of which have been verified.

Another striking similarity of the visions is that the messages given by Mary to the children are always the same. For instance, at the Immaculate Conception at Lourdes in 1858, Our Holy Mother said: "Penitence! Penitence! Penitence! You're to pray to God for sinners. Go and kiss the ground in penance for the conversion of sinners."

At our Lady of Carmel, Garabandal, October 18, 1961, the Virgin said: "We must do much penance and make many sacrifices. We must often visit the Blessed Sacrament. But, above all, we must be very good, for if we are not, we will be punished..."

At Palmer de Troya, Spain, April 25, 1971: "Many times I have told you 'Obey your pastors,' but now I will tell you 'Obey your pastors in that which is fundamental...'"

The message, as you can see, is very nearly the same in every instance. The impression is that Mary is doing a lot more than simply admonishing us—she is trying to warn us. The question now that begs to be answered is: Warn us of what? Impending doom?

Sister Lucy's Startling Statement

If you have wondered why Mary is coming to us so frequently, you may have an answer in the words of Sister Lucy, who spoke them in 1961, one year after the "secret message" was supposed to have been released.

Sister Lucy said: "It is already time that each one of us accomplishes holy deeds of his own initiative and reforms his life according to Our Lady's appeal...She told me that when the other means are exhausted and despised by men, she is giving us the last anchor of salvation, that is the Holy Virgin in person..."

The words are clear, the meaning unmistakable. Lucy tells us that Mary is trying desperately to save us by making her appearances as often as she can. The visions are our last hope. Obviously, she prays that her appearance will jolt us into mending our ways. It is her last resort. Every other method has been despised and exhausted. In the coming years, we are likely to see many more visions of Mary as she works tirelessly in her efforts to save mankind.

Mary in Alien Lands

Oddly enough, Mary has appeared in countries which are not in accord with Christian beliefs. One of those places is Russia. In 1948, a local secretary of the communist party, a man named Liaret, saw a tall figure in the road ahead of him. He called her the "lady in night."

Also in 1948, in Trieste, a young girl saw a beautiful angel who told her to return to the same spot every day for fifteen days. The girl did so, seeing the same vision on every occasion. At the end of the period the girl was given seven perfect rose petals. A botanist examined the petals and stated emphatically that they had not come from any roses grown on earth.

In a Catholic country, Italy, in 1947, a communist sympathizer in Tre Fontane saw an angel-like figure which appeared to be the Virgin Mary. Thousands of people visited the spot, and many of them were communists who later rejected their atheistic beliefs.

The Holy Mother has been seen in virtually every country in the world, regardless of that nation's religious or political beliefs. Apparently, she appears before us not to make converts, but to awaken us to the fact that time may be running out.

Jose Daniel Cruz took this photo of what he says is an apparition of the Virgin Mary who appeared at the Holy Mountain a popular spot for visions in Puerto Rico.

24 Ways Mary Presents Herself

A Methodist clergyman in Haines City, Florida, Reverend B.W. Palmer, has spent years collecting hundreds of contemporary visions of the Holy Mother. His research on the subject indicates that there are at least 24 methods the Virgin uses to manifest herself. There may be as many as fifty ways, but we list here the 24 most commonly manifested.

1. The skies appear to open up and Mary with a band of angels appears to descend.

2. In the presence of a viewer, Mary appears to descend in a shaft of light.

3. The Virgin appears or disappears through a solid object such as a door or a wall.

4. A viewer may hear footsteps outside his house. Then a knock on the door. When he opens it he sees the Holy Mother.

5. The Virgin can also appear as though she is in a picture on the wall.

6. A witness may awake because he feels a spiritual presence in the room, or may feel someone's touch. When he opens his eyes he sees the Holy Figure bending over him.

7. An angel or the spirit of a deceased person may appear to the witness first, then lead him to the materialization of the Holy Mother.

8. The witness may see the face of the Virgin or Jesus Christ appear above the person who is desperately in need of help.

9. The witness may hear a voice which tells him or her to go to a certain place and do a certain thing. When he complies, he sees the Virgin Mary.

10. The figure of the Virgin Mary appears in the sky, but greatly magnified.

11. The viewer may be awakened by the light of a very bright moon. At that moment he sees the Holy Mother.

12. Clouds play a part in visions. The Virgin often appears out of a cloud moving toward a person, and she also uses the cloud to make her departure.

13. A cloud or heavy mist may materialize in the viewer's room. And out of the mist the Virgin will appear.

14. During the Fatima miracle, the Holy Mother appeared to the three children in exactly the same way. All three gave the same description of what they saw. In many cases the Virgin appears to several persons at the same time, but each witness gave a different description of what he or she saw. To one witness, the Holy Mother may appear as a ball of light; to another, a flash of lightning; to another, a disembodied voice.

15. The Virgin may appear in a room occupied by several people. But only one person will see her. The others may see the spirits of the dead.

16. The Virgin may also appear in the dreams of a witness. A manifestation like this is usually associated with healing or cures.

17. The Holy Mother may vanish suddenly, or fade away slowly, slipping into a cloud, through the ceiling, doors or walls. She may walk away, fading from view as she gets further and further away from the witness.

18. In most visions of the Holy Mother, only the witness singled out for communications may see her even though there are a lot of people present. This was so in the Fatima miracle in which thousands of people saw the three children talking to an entity they could not see.

19. In many of the visions collected by Rev. Palmer, the Virgin appears in a strange light, one that illuminates the wit-

ness as well. In some of these cases, the light appeared first, then the Holy Figure.

20. In some visions, the witnesses said they saw no figures at all, but were aware of the Holy Presences through the supernatural light and the voices that came to them.

21. Those who have experienced out-of-body incidents have reported seeing the Holy Mother, but that the vision disappeared once the out-of-body experience ended.

22. In other out-of-body experiences, people have claimed to travel through space to visit friends and relatives, and on such excursions have usually seen a Holy Figure, that is, the Holy Mother, a saint, an angel, or other Holy Entities.

23. In still other out-of-body travels, people have claimed to have seen the lower spirit worlds where good spirits attempt to help the lower spirits. In some instances during these lower-plane visits, the travelers have seen Jesus Christ or the Virgin Mary.

24. During near-death experiences, people said they saw Jesus or Mary for a brief moment when their bodies were physically dead.

This material originally appeared in Brad Steiger's book, Gods of Aquarius, *published in paperback by Berkley.*

Mary's predictions often deal with a fiery "Ball of Redemption" which She says will strike Earth if humankind does not give up its evil ways.

Mary's Miracle of the Nuns

Under the Tsars of Russia the Russian Orthodox Church was permitted to have convents. But during the 1920s the Communists liquidated them. The last to be crushed were the convents in Ruthenia in the Ukraine in 1949. Three of the nuns were sent to a concentration camp in Vorkuta, where temperatures dropped to 50 degrees below zero Fahrenheit.

The nuns were ordered to make bricks. They refused to do so. They told the foreman that working for the Communists was the same as working for the devil. The nuns said they were servants of God, not Satan, and they would not carry out the order no matter what happened to them.

They were immediately stripped of their habits and placed on starvation rations, which consisted of black bread and rancid soup.

Day after day they were ordered to go to the brick factory or the clay pits, but they refused. The nuns were not naive. They knew their refusal meant that they would be tortured, perhaps to the point of death. And they were right.

The commandant of the camp ordered the three nuns to be placed in strait jackets. But that was not all. Their arms were tied behind them. The rope that bound their hands was then passed around their ankles and drawn up tight, so that their feet were pulled up behind them and their back wrenched arc-like. The position was one of excruciating pain.

The nuns were in agony, but they did not cry out or beg for mercy. The commandant then ordered that water be poured over them so that the cotton material of the strait jackets would shrink, creating more pressure on their tortured bodies. He waited for them to cry out, to beg, to ask for forgiveness. But all that happened was that the nuns passed out.

The bonds were loosened. After some time went by, the torture began again, and again the nuns lapsed into unconsciousness. The commandant then ordered the torture to stop. He needed the nuns alive to work making bricks. They had been tormented almost to the point of death, and he was certain now that they had learned their lesson and would obey orders.

And we know from what happened later that Mother Mary was watching this abomination and was preparing to act.

Mary's Prophecy to the Nuns

The commandant was furious. He ordered that the nuns be taken to the work detail. If they refused to work, they were to be taken to a ridge and made to stand still in the freezing cold and watch the others work.

The women of God would not work. A moment later they found themselves on a high hill, without gloves or caps, and exposed to the full fury of the biting wind. Instead of standing, however, they knelt in prayer.

Below them, scores of women chipped away at mud bricks to make them ready for the ovens. They suffered from the cold, but knew that their stubborn sisters on the hummock above them would surely freeze to death. The nuns were not properly dressed for the weather. They had no gloves. Their heads were bare. They were doomed to freeze to death in the Arctic weather.

By order of the commandant, the nuns were to remain exposed to the elements for eight hours, the length of the working day. He knew that by that time the women would be dead, frozen solid.

What he did not know was that the three nuns had a vision while on the ridge. It was Mary. She seemed suspended in mid-air. She told the women that they would not be cold, and that they would not die on the ridge because of their faith in God.

After dark, some guards climbed the hill, expecting to find three corpses. Instead, the women seemed relaxed and warm! The guards were shocked. They escorted the women to the barracks and hurried to the commandant to tell him what happened.

The commandant coldly ordered that the nuns have their shawls removed the next day and that they were again to stand on the ridge for eight hours.

Mary's Second Visit

The second day saw the three nuns without caps, gloves or shawls and subjected to the fierce Siberian winter. As soon as they were taken to the same ridge they knelt in prayer and told their guards that they would remain kneeling for the next eight hours.

Sometime during the long day Mother Mary appeared to the resolute women. She told them to remain stout-hearted, that She would protect them.

When guards came for them that evening they were surprised to find them warm and not at all uncomfortable because of the weather. In the barracks, the guards looked for frost-bite on the women's hands, feet, ears and faces, but could find no signs of it!

The Third Day

This time the commandant ordered the nuns' scarves removed. This was done and again the women withstood the freezing cold. Allegedly, the weather on the third day was one of the coldest on record in the Vorkuta. Yet the women survived with no bad effects. They were returned to the barracks just as healthy as they had ever been.

By this time, the news of what was happening had spread to all of the camps in the Vorkuta region. Whenever the other women saw the nuns they blessed themselves. They were aware of the fact that a miracle was taking place. Everyone in the Vorkuta region was talking about the incident. Even the secret police came to the camp to look at the nuns on the hill. The commandant, not a religious man, was disturbed. He felt that a power not of this earth had taken a hand in this affair.

The Fourth Day

The guards were so fearful now that they absolutely refused to have anything to do with the nuns. They would not touch them or even go near them. The commandant was suddenly gripped with fear, and would not order the nuns to the hill. Further, the nuns were permitted to pray. They were taken off their starvation rations and were not ordered to work. They spent the next four years in the camp preparing their own food and making their own clothes. They were regarded with awe and respect. The guards were told to leave them alone. The nuns carried out their devotions in their own way and were at peace. They were still prisoners, but they were spiritually free...thanks to Mother Mary!

At the site of many Marian miracles in Secedah, Wisconsin, this Our Lady of Fatima statue was photographed lifting Her head and smiling. The picture was taken by the son of Mrs. Mary Ann Van Hoff with a small Brownie camera and was only seen after the film was printed. The picture on the left is the original form of Our Lady's statue. (Photo courtesy of Brother Vincent de Paul, T.S.O.F., of the Immaculate Heart.)

Mother Mary's Prophecy About America

The date was November 12, 1949. The time: 11:00 p.m. The city: Necedah, Wisconsin. Mrs. Mary Ann Van Hoof was in her bed when she heard a rustling sound in the next room. When she looked up she saw a dim figure moving toward her. Mary Ann trembled with fear. She turned away, too frightened to look. When she did steal a glance, the figure was gone.

The woman said nothing about the experience for nearly a month. When she finally told her family, the consensus was that she had been visited by the Virgin Mary.

It wasn't until April 7, 1950, Good Friday, that Mary Ann received a second visit from the Holy Mother. It was late, 11:00 o'clock. She was in bed. Suddenly, a sweet womanly voice said, "My child."

Mary Ann looked up. There was nothing. Yet the voice apparently came from the Crucifix on the wall. Christ's body was shining and it appeared to be twice its normal size. The voice said, "I was with you last November 12. Pray, my child—pray hard! Your cross is heavy to bear. But the people all over the world are facing a much heavier cross of sorrow, because of the enemy of God—unless we pray. Pray hard, and with all of your heart. Pray devotedly. Nightly Rosary precisely at eight o'clock."

Mother Mary Instructs Her Listener

"Ask your pastor, the father of his parish, to tell his people, children of God, to pray the Rosary every evening at eight o'clock, no matter what happens! Because prayer only will help you. Tell this to your relatives and to your husband's relatives. Yes, you are frightened, but don't be. My child, you will be laughed at with disbelief, and many will say things against you. When your mission is fulfilled, I will be back. Not in this room, but outside, by the flowers when the trees and grass are green. I give you my blessing. May God bless you!"

The voice was gone. Mary Ann had not seen the figure of Mary. She stared at the Crucifixion, which now stopped shining and regained its normal size.

Mary Ann did as she was instructed, and the Rosary Mission was made by a few of the faithful. In fact, it is still being made, often in weather that is 30 degrees below zero.

On Pentecost Sunday, May 28, 1950, Mary Ann was in her kitchen about noon when she looked out her window at four ash trees in her backyard. They were about 50 feet from the house. Suddenly, there was a flash of light. Then a strange ball of blue mist appeared and moved from behind an ash tree to the top branches. Mary Ann didn't know it at the time, but Mother Mary's method here was the same one she used in Fatima, Portugal, when she appeared before the three blessed children.

Mary Ann left her kitchen and walked toward the mist, fascinated and unafraid. She stared hard, waiting. Then a form began to take shape. The Queen of Heaven appeared! She stood in a white cloud, aglow, the white aura around her studded with roses. She descended from atop the tree to merely a short height above the ground. She wore her Rosary.

The Queen of the Holy Rosary told Mary Ann not to be frightened. She asked the woman to mark the spot of the vision with a cross. Mary Ann looked around for an object. The Holy Mother said, "Dig in the ground and you will find a rock."

51

Mary Ann did so and found a rock, which she used to mark a cross on the ground.

Mary Ann was told: "Go to mass and receive Holy Communion for 15 days. You must also fast—eat only enough to equal one meal a day for 15 days. Also, go to mass on the next five first Saturdays, in honor of my Immaculate Heart.

The Virgin Mary was aware of the physical pains that afflicted Mary Ann and which had been with her ever since she heard Mother Mary's voice come to her from the Crucifixion in her room. Mary Ann was told: "You will continue to suffer those pains for sinners. Tomorrow, bring your Rosary and a lilac blossom. And then I shall give you further instructions for the priests and all of the people. Your heart is heavy now, so go, my child, and I bless you."

Before the vision faded, the Holy Mother told Mary Ann that she would see her the next day and the day after that. (These three days are now called "Mary Days" by the faithful.) The Holy Mother also told Mary Ann that she would be with her every year on June 4, which is Trinity Sunday, and June 15, the feast of the Sacred Heart, and August 15, the Feast of the Most Holy Rosary.

Strange Sight of Rosary is Witnessed

The next day, May 29, 1950, Mary Ann took her Rosary and a lilac blossom to the holy place in her backyard. Again she saw the blue mist and saw the vision of the Virgin Mary. Our Lady smiled at her and said, "You are not frightened at all today."

She was right. Mary Ann was too full of wonder to be frightened. Our Lady said: "Mary Ann, do you still wish to bring my message to the people? Know that if you agree, you will then be ridiculed and laughed at with disbelief, suffering unkind persecution."

At this point, Mary Ann's son, Fred, and her daughter, Jo Ann, were watching their mother from the kitchen window. Of course, they saw only their mother. They did not see the Holy Mother or the blue mist.

At the Sacred Spot, the vision reached down and took Mary Ann's Rosary and touched it to her own Rosary. The two astonished children saw their mother's Rosary suspended in mid-air! Of course, Our Lady was holding the Rosary, but the children couldn't see her. They then saw the Rosary come back into their mother's hands!

Mary's Warning About America

After Our Lady told Mary Ann that she wanted a priest to bless the Sacred Spot where she appeared, she said: "I want America to wake up! The enemy of God is creeping all over America. Don't believe that it can't happen here. I am warning you people, again, just as I warned people at LaSalette, France, at Fatima, Portugal, and at Lipa, Philippines, of what did happen, and what will yet happen. Still, the people believe me not, and the people have no faith in me. The people turn their backs on me. Write to the Vicar of Christ to give him this message." (The message was sent to Pope Pius XII on June 8, 1950.)

Mary then said: "On October 7, I shall give you your final penance. You will be spared only if effort is made to do what I ask, and I am satisfied. At Fatima, it took nearly 30 years. It must not take 30 years now. It will be too late. Only the vigil of prayer will save the destruction of the world."

During the vision of May 30, Our Lady said: "Remember, my child, the time is coming when sorrow and slaughter of my children will be the worst than ever in history." (The Actual destruction of America was shown to Mary Ann on June 16, 1950.)

Mary said: "It grieves me to see innocent children, the sick, and the poor, destroyed because of greed, and the desire of power, by a few nations' leaders. That is why I say, 'Pray, pray. Give this message to the world, for only prayer will save the destruction of the people."

The Trials of Mary Ann

Our Holy Mother appeared on Trinity Sunday. Her opening words to Mary Ann were: "Bless you, my child, and your 28 helping friends." (This figure was accurate.) "This pleases me. Bless them with the crucifix of your Rosary. (This was the Rosary that touched the one held by Our Lady.) Place it on their foreheads and say, 'Bless you. This blessing is from me.'"

The Holy Mother then begged Mary Ann to tell the school children to pray. She said: "Pray for the children for a cleaner life. Put clean thoughts into their minds. And tell them to have devotion to my Son. Teach them sacrifices, penances and prayers for sinners."

It is not known if Mary Ann carried out these instructions. If she failed to do so, there were good reasons. Mary Ann was a hard working farm woman. She had seven children to care for and a large house to tend to. Many of her friends said that the woman had the afflictions of Job.

Worse, tragedy and disaster struck that year. On February 7, her large house burned to the ground during a cold snap when the temperature dipped to 40 degrees below zero.

She then had a vision of her son being killed in an auto accident. Later, it happened exactly the way she saw it. Then her husband died, and later a man named Henry Swan, who was her protector, also died.

Despite all of her hardships, Mary Ann never failed to keep her appointments with Our Lady. On one occasion, Mary Ann begged the Holy Mother to show herself to a priest. The answer was, "Bless you, my child," and the vision faded.

Mystery of the Scapular

The vision of October 7, 1950 was somewhat different from the others. This time, Mary Ann gave a detailed description of what the Holy Mother was wearing, and it is well worth including here because it tells about the mystery of the Scapular.

Mary Ann said: "Our Holy Mother was dressed in blue— the symbol of piety, and there was a large Rosary circled above her. The circle was tilted so that it was higher than her head in the front and lower in the back. The circle was much wider than her shoulders.

"The cross of the Rosary hung down almost as far as her left shoulder. The medal of the Rosary showed Our Lady of Mount Carmel, holding the brown Scapular. The cross and medal were gold. The beads were about as big as baseballs, and they seemed to be transparent, so that the color that was behind them showed through. This color is hard to describe. It was something like—all the colors of the rainbow, and they seemed to be turning and shooting out rays of light."

This description can be found nowhere else, in no other vision. Mary Ann was privileged on this single occasion to see clearly the minute details of the vision.

It was important, too, to note the presence of the brown Scapular being held by Our Lady of Mount Carmel. The Scapular was the first Sacramental that Our Lady gave to the world, in 1204, when she presented it to St. Simon Stock of Saragossa, Spain.

Our Lady has promised that all who are enrolled in this Scapular by a priest, and wear it at his death after a life of chastity, will be released from Purgatory on the first Saturday following death. Our Lady died on a Saturday, and this is the possible reason for her selection of Saturday. Her resurrection and bodily ascension came on the morning of the next day, Sunday.

The reference to Purgatory here implies salvation, and that the wearer who fulfills the conditions, will not be condemned to hell. The holy words on the Scapular read: "He who dies clothed in this Scapular will never see Hellfire."

Miracle of the Sun in Wisconsin

During one of her appearances before Mary Ann, the Holy Mother said that she would perform a miracle on October 17, 1950. Although newspapers did not carry the story, word got around by word of mouth, and when the day came, more than 100,000 people showed up in Necedah, Wisconsin. Incredibly, they came from all over the United States., Canada, Mexico and even from the Philippines.

All of these people saw the sun leave its position in the sky. Just as in Fatima in 1917, the viewers were able to look directly at the scene without harming their eyes. And they watched while the bright orb spun around and shot out brilliant colors across the sky. The phenomenon began when everyone was saying the Rosary. Many stopped praying to snap photographs. All stood in awe when they saw the great Cross of Light. A bishop from Medford fell down and kissed the ground. People blessed themselves, their eyes riveted to the wonder in the sky. Many of the witnesses are still living in Necedah and enjoy describing what happened that day. There, they call it the "Sun Miracle."

Saints Visit Mary Ann Van Hoof

The woman saw the Holy Mother, as we stated before, at four ash trees in her back yard. On one occasion, St. Michael the Archangel made a visit and bent those four ash trees to the ground. Today, those trees, once straight up, are now bent, two to the left and two to the right.

Besides the Blessed Virgin Mary, the woman has seen visions of St. Joseph, St. Theresa, St. Ann, St. Francis, St. Joan of Arc, St. Clare, the unknown saint called St. Philomena, Tsar Alexander Romanov III of Russia, St. Hegesippus and St. Dymphna.

Miracles of the Rosary

Many pilgrims standing and praying at the Sacred Spot in Mary Ann's back yard stated that their Rosaries changed to gold. Others have stated that their Rosary beads changed color.

One Rosary that was changed to gold was taken to Firmin Desloge, St. Louis University and touched to the lips of two people who were unconscious from accidents. One was a 19-year-old girl who was in a coma for four weeks. The other was a middle-aged man unconscious for three days because of an industrial accident. Both opened their eyes and began to speak as soon as their lips were touched!

Mother Mary's Incredible Prophecy

The date was March 26, 1954 when Our Lady told Mary Ann something about chemical and biological warfare—not the kind in which front-line soldiers wear gas masks—but a far different kind, one that will creep into every living being on earth.

"Products are infected with radioactivity, for distribution among nations. The enemy is using this as a means of destroying stomachs. This new disease will be called a new sort of cancer. It will spring up in many countries, including the United States. It is not a natural cancer. It is man-made. It will destroy many. This is why you must pray like you never prayed before. Only prayer will avert this catastrophe and make it a lesser illness."

The Quiet Bomb

During the same vision, Mother Mary said: "Grief and sorrow! Man is planning on making a bomb of poison. When it falls upon the earth, whatever it touches will die! All living things. The only thing that will keep them from using this one, is fear of destroying themselves. Pray, children, pray that God's Hand will reach out and protect you before man goes completely mad with the greed and want of power. Those in control of this think they are God, and there is no other God."

3. (Above) August 1917 — The little Seers in te patio of the home of the parents of Jacinta and Francisco

(Below) September 1917 — The three little Shepherds before the holmoak on which Our Lady appeared

Mystery of Mary's Five Secret Messages

As we said earlier, Mary is likely to appear anywhere in the world. It doesn't make any difference if the nation is God-fearing or Godless. And during the afternoon of June 24, 1981, Our Lady made a startling appearance to six youngsters in Yugoslavia, a communist-controlled country.

The particular area was on the hill of Podbrdo on Mount Krisevach near Medjugorje. The privileged young people were four girls: Vida Ivankovich, 17; Mijana Dragicevich, 16; Mirija Paulovich, 16; Ivanka Ivankovish, 15; and two boys: Ivan Dragicevich, 16; and Jacov Colo, 10.

All of them described the vision in the same way—that the Lady was clad in gray and wore a white veil. She appeared to be suspended above the ground.

Jacov, the youngest, fell to his knees and the others then did the same. The Mother of God told the children that her greatest joy would be to see peace everywhere in the world. She asked them to pray and to do penance for that peace, to go to the sacraments frequently, and to put their trust in God.

When Mother Mary asked them to listen carefully, that she was about to entrust them with five secret messages which had to be given personally to the Pope and to no one else!

The children received the messages, and when the vision vanished, they rushed to Father Josip Zovko in the Franciscan parish rectory.

The six children told the priest about the vision, but insisted that they keep Mary's secrets for the Pope's ears only.

In the days that followed, the children went to the same hilltop every afternoon and saw the Blessed Virgin. She spoke to them almost every day. It was to be expected that the great news would spread throughout the region. In no time at all large crowds stood behind the six children, hoping that they too would see the apparition. That was not to be, but the people did fall to their knees and pray.

Although many of the people badgered the children about the secret messages, they stuck to their guns and would not reveal them.

Miracles Occur

A blind man somehow made his way to the hilltop, alone and unaided. He fell to his knees and prayed along with everyone else, but when he stood up again he could see! His eyesight was completely restored!

A paralyzed child was brought to the hill. Later, she was able to walk home, unaided! Many others who were sick were healed after visiting the site of Mary's appearance. What disturbed the communist leaders more than anything else, however, were the vast numbers of people who converted to Catholicism. Actually, that was the greatest miracle because it was a religious awakening in an area, Medjugorje, where religion had been successfully suppressed.

A Holy Man Speaks and the Mystery Deepens

A priest who visited the hilltop, spoke to the six children, saw the miracles, and listened to the Franciscan priests, spoke later about his experiences. He lives in Yugoslavia and therefore is reluctant to use his name. He is not in Yugoslavia now, and if he used his name in connection with what he said, he would be deprived of re-entry into his country and would be declared an undesirable alien by the communists. This is what he said:

"How can I evaluate my experience at Medjugorje? It was a time of great grace for me personally. Certainly I feel closer to Mary, more aware of her love in my priestly life. I know that somehow I am closer to her now and more of a priest.

"How do I evaluate what has happened and what is still going on at Medjugorgje? The Church has not spoken officially and like any Catholic I will conform my personal evaluation to the Church's authoritative pronouncement when that comes.

"Personally, though, I have no doubts as to the validity of the apparitions. Any doubts I might have had were removed by what I saw and heard, especially by the powerful spirit of holiness, of reverence, of prayer."

According to the anonymous priest quoted above, the five secret messages have not yet been delivered to Pope John Paul. No one knows what they are, but the publisher of this book has committed himself to make them known to his readers as soon as they are released to the world.

Fact's About Mary's Appearances

Our Lady is nearly always consistent when she makes an appearance. The fact is that Mary almost always appears to children or adults who are simple and innocent. She does not appear to the world-wise sophisticates. Many of the people privileged to see her are uneducated. It is as though she selects a clean slate on which to write her messages. The little people, the humble, the poor, the unlearned and illiterate are more likely to accept the apparition as true. The people with cluttered minds, and those who cling to pretentious philosophies, are poor receivers. Were they fortunate enough to receive messages from Mary, they would undoubtedly twist them, or question them, or even negate them and not pass them on.

Still another fact is that Mary always appears accompanied by a brilliant light. There is no exception to this. The light has an unearthly intensity, yet it does not hurt the eyes of those who witness the apparition. In the Fatima vision, when Francesco was questioned about the brightness of the light given off by the Virgin, he said: "The figure of the Virgin was brighter than the sun." Juan Diego at Guadalupe told of golden beams that rayed from Mary's body from head to foot.

Another characteristic common to all visions is that Our Lady always appears young and beautiful. Her youth in the apparitions represents a fresh new life of salvation for mankind. Our Lady also appears in white gowns. Witnesses have also seen blue and gold, but the dominating color is white.

Mary's War With Satan

We don't think of Mary as having to face opposition when she decides to make an appearance. Actually, she does, and from a formidable foe—Satan. When you recount the problems which have arisen before and during Mary's apparitions, you can only wonder that the Devil is working furiously to prevent her from reaching the people.

A case in point concerns the night before the last great message was to be received from Fatima. The entire continent of Europe was swept by a storm of such great intensity that William Thomas Walsh wrote in his book, *Our Lady*: "It was as if the Devil, somewhere in the ice and snow that could never slake the burning of his pain, had resolved to destroy with one blow all that remained of the Europe which had so long been his battleground against the Thing he hated most."

And we know that when the sun fell from the sky at Fatima, there had been a driving downpour for hours. Everyone was soaked, yet when the sun returned to its rightful position in the sky, all 70,000 spectators noted that their clothes were dry.

Several visions at Banneux took place in the driving rain. At Lourdes, the weather was so cold that Bernadette was not allowed to gather wood with her playmates. The water Bernadette had to cross to reach Lourdes was extremely cold. The same water on her return, however, was warm. And at Knock, Ireland, spectators had to stand in pouring rain during a vision. The ground at the spot where the apparition took place was perfectly dry.

Obviously, the war of good against evil extends even to Mary's attempts to reach us. Satan tries desperately hard to stand between the Holy Virgin and her children. Fortunately, for us, Mary always succeeds in her fight against him.

Mary's Messages Are Pleas

In most cases, the Virgin Mary begs, pleads and cajoles us to listen to her. The messages are always clear and direct. Her theme is that God is displeased with what is happening here on Earth, and she begs us to mend our ways. Her message at La Salette was: "If my people will not obey, I shall be compelled to loose my Son's arm. It is so heavy, so pressing, that I can no longer restrain it. How long have I suffered for you! If my Son is not to cast you off, I am obliged to entreat Him without ceasing."

Mary's Prophecies Always Come True

History proves that every time Mary made a prediction, it became a reality. She told St. Catherine Laboure that there would be revolutions in France in 1830 and in 1848. Both upheavals came to pass. When she appeared at La Salette she said that would be a great famine. It happened not long after. At Fatima, Mary predicted World War II and the spread of communism throughout the world.

Mary's Promise of Hope

Our Lady has made startling predictions which have yet to materialize. One is that her Son will return to earth in the 1980s. Another is that Russia will be converted. This holds great significance for all of us who dread the coming of a thermonuclear war. The two great powers, the United States and Russia, have the capability of destroying the entire planet. Will it happen? History shows that the thought of genocide and mass destruction have never before prevented war. However, Mother Mary holds positive hope. She tells us: "If my requests are heard, Russia will be converted and there will be peace. But in the end my Immaculate Heart will triumph. I will convert sinners."

This is the hope we must cling to, that Mary will triumph over evil.

Let us now examine the great visions of Mary, the miracles she wrought, and the promises she made.

Virgin of Guadalupe, Mexico (Chapter begins next page).

Mother Mary At Guadalupe, Mexico

The vision occurred at the top of a 130-foot hill in a wasteland about five miles north of Mexico City. The date was December 9, 1531, a Saturday. The time was daybreak. The man who saw the apparition was an Aztec Indian named Nahuati or Singing Eagle. He was a poor man who lived in obscurity. Yet he would become famous and known to millions almost over night and without benefit of radio and television. His wife was dead and there were no children. He had an uncle. He and the uncle were converted by Franciscan missionaries and given new names. Singing Eagle was now Juan Diego. The uncle was Juan Bernadino.

On the day in question, Juan Diego left his village of Tolpetlac before dawn to go to Mass, which celebrated Our Lady's honor, in the church of Santiago in Tlaltelolco. He had to run because he didn't want to be late. But suddenly he stopped. He heard birds singing. Normally, he would have kept going, but this was not the time of year to hear birds. It was too bleak and cold. Yet now, the music the birds made was sweet, and he seemed to hear choirs of birdsong all around him. Then quite suddenly, the birds stopped, totally. There was only silence now.

The next strange thing to happen was the sound of a woman's voice, calling: "Juan! Juanito!" She was apparently on top of Tepeyac hill. Juan couldn't see her. He started up the hill, feeling that she must be in trouble.

The sun was not yet above the horizon, yet now he saw a girl who radiated golden beams from her head to her feet, just as though she stood with her back to the sun. She appeared to be a Mexican girl about 14 and exceedingly beautiful.

The Girls Speaks

The lovely young woman said: "Juan, smallest and dearest of my little children, where are you going?"

Juan replied: "I was hurrying to see the Mass and hear the Gospel explained."

The girl said: "Dear little son, I love you. I want you to know who I am. I am the ever-virgin Mary, Mother of the true God who gives life and maintains it in existence. He created all things. He is in all places. He is lord of heaven and earth. I desire a teocali (shrine or church) at this place where I will show my compassion to your people and to all people who sincerely ask my help in their work and in their sorrows. Here, I will see their tears; I will console them and they will be at ease. So run now to Tenochtitlan (Mexico City) and tell the Lord Bishop all that you have seen and heard."

Juan Diego, now prostrate, rose quickly and said he would do as the Holy Mother asked.

Juan Diego had no trouble running the five miles to Mexico City. Where he did find trouble was trying to convince the Lord Bishop, Fray Juan de Zumarraga, that he had seen the vision of the Virgin Mary and that she requested the building of a shrine at the spot where she appeared.

Juan tried for two days to convince the bishop but failed. Or thought he did. The bishop finally said to him that if Santa Maria could give him a sign to prove that she had made an appearance, then the bishop would believe him.

The Virgin Mary's Sign

Juan Diego hurried back to the hill on which he had seen the vision. He waited there, and soon the apparition appeared.

Juan told her what had happened. Mary said: "Very well, little son. Come back tomorrow at daybreak. I will give you a sign for him. You have taken much trouble on my account, and I shall reward you for it. Go in peace and rest."

But there was no peace and rest for Juan Diego. When he returned to his village he learned that his uncle, Juan Bernadino, was desperately ill. He was stricken with cocolistle, a deadly fever.

Juan stayed with his uncle all night. He was supposed to see the Virgin Mary at dawn, but knew he couldn't make it. Then his uncle took a turn for the worse. He asked his nephew to get a priest from Mexico City. The older man knew he was dying.

Juan obeyed him. He ran out of the village and headed for the hills that would take him to Mexico City. That was when he saw the Virgin Mary coming toward him. He was glad to see her, but this was the wrong time. He had to fetch a priest in a hurry. He had no time to listen to Mary.

Nevertheless, she stopped him and asked him why he was in such a hurry. He said, "My uncle is dying of cocolistle and I must get a priest for him."

The Blessed Virgin said, "My little son, do not be distressed and afraid. Am I not her who am your Mother? Are you not under my shadow and protection? Your uncle will not die this time. This very moment his health is restored. There is no reason now for the errand you set out on, and you can peacefully attend to mind. Go to the top of the hill; cut the flowers that are growing there and bring them to me."

Juan Diego did not question the Holy Mother, but he knew perfectly well that flowers could not grow at this time of year; it was much too cold. He also knew that his uncle could not be cured so quickly. He was wasting away when Juan left him.

Juan climbed the hill and found lovely Castilian roses growing out of the earth. It was impossible! Yet, there they were! When he cut them he noticed that they were drenched with dew. But all around them, the scrub and mesquite were rimed with frost.

Juan protected the delicate flowers by wrapping them in his tilma, which was an Aztec garment worn like a long cloak. But his arrangement was wrong. Mary took the flowers out of the tilma and carefully placed each one inside the garment so that they would not spill out during his trip to the Lord Bishop.

She told Juan: "You see, little son, this is the sign I am sending to the Bishop. Tell him that now he has his sign, he should build the temple I desire in this place. Do not let anyone but him see what you are carrying. Tell him about your uncle being desperately ill and that now he is healed. Tell him that I sent you to cut these roses and that I arranged them myself. You are my trusted ambassador, and this time the Bishop will believe all that you tell him."

Juan Diego didn't know it at the time, but he would never again see the Virgin Mary all his life.

Mary's Greater Sign

Juan finally stood before the Lord Bishop and told his incredible story. Then he unwrapped his tilma and let the flowers topple to the floor. The Bishop bolted to his feet! Awe was written across his face. He did not look at the flowers; instead, he stared hard at the tilma, for on it was the glorious image of Juan's vision. It was the Holy Mother! The imprint was clear and distinct, a picture no artist could have drawn.

The Lord Bishop fell to his knees before the miraculous picture and prayed. Then he rose, took the tilma from Juan and attached it to a wall near the altar.

Juan Diego was quite satisfied. Mary had given the Bishop two signs. What's more, his uncle was cured by a miracle. And now Juan would return to his village and see about building the shrine to the Holy Mother. But he did not return alone. An army of priests went with him, for the news about Juan's vision had spread quickly. The villagers were waiting for him outside his uncle's house. Juan Bernadino was sitting in the sun, looking quite healthy, when his nephew approached. They embraced to the cheers of the crowd.

68

Uncle Juan's Vision

The older man told his nephew that the night before, when he was too weak to drink the herbal tea beside him, and when he was certain he would die, he saw the room fill with a soft light. A beautiful woman materialized out of nothing and she stood beside him. She told Juan Bernadino that she saw his nephew and sent him to the Lord Bishop with a picture of herself on Juan's tilma. She told the man he would get well. Then she said, "Call me and call my image Santa Maria de Guadalupe." A moment later she disappeared.

Millions Converted

From 1532 to 1538, eight million natives were baptized. In one five-day period shortly after Juan's last vision, 14,500 showed up at Friar Toribio de Benavente's mission and were annointed with oil and chrism. When the natives learned about the sacrament of marriage, 1,000 of them were married in one day. During Easter time, 1,540 natives from 12 different tribes assembled at one church. Some traveled more than 150 miles!

Today, more than five million come annually to worship at the shrine.

Miracle of the Tilma

Today, Juan Diego's tilma can still be seen above the high altar in the beautifully domed church, built in honor of Santa Maria de Guadalupe. The tilma consists of two straight pieces coarsely woven of fibre from the maguey plant. They are sewn together, so that the whole measures 66 inches by 41 inches. It looks like unbleached linen.

Scientists tell us that in Mexico's hot climate, the tilma should have disintegrated 20 years after it was made!

They also tell us that because of its fishnet-like web, no one could have painted on it. And even if a properly prepared canvas had been used, the painting would have lasted no more than 200 years. After that it would have browned over to such an extent that it would have been obliterated.

The colors and gilt remain a mystery. The technique defies copying. The tilma is as good now as it was more than 400 years ago. The conclusion among church authorities is that Mary watches over it with care. Devotees are convinced the tilma will never disintegrate.

Mary's figure on the tilma is 56 inches tall. Up close, it looks small. When you draw away from it, it seems to grow larger. The golden rays that Juan Diego saw around the vision are represented on the tilma. She is exactly as Juan saw her.

Juan Diego saw her as a person of his own race, and the image bears this out. Her star-studded mantle is like that of an Aztec queen.

Miracle of the Exploding Bomb

In 1921 the leaders of the Mexico government were persecutors of the church. The church of the Santa Maria de Guadalupe, however, were not closed because government officials were afraid that doing so would cause an uprising from the Indian masses.

They were probably right. But someone brought a bunch of flowers into the church and placed them at the altar. No one saw him enter or leave. Inside the flowers was a large bomb. It was timed to go off at the end of a pontifical high Mass.

Many important church dignitaries were present. The church was packed with worshippers. At the end of the Mass the bomb went off with a deafening explosion. And Mary performed still another miracle. No one was hurt. An altarpiece was shattered and a huge bronze cross twisted. But the tilma and image on it were not even scratched!

Yes, Mary had worked a miracle, for the size of the bomb should have destroyed a great many lives and injured hundreds more.

But it was not to be. Like the image on the tilma that is not of man's making, and not of this earth, so too was the ineffectiveness of the bomb, which was not of this world....

There are now hundreds of documented cases of Mary appearing in this century to believers and non-believers alike.

The Strange Story of Catherine Laboure

Catherine Laboure was born on May 2, 1806, in the village of Ain-les-moutiers, not far from Dijon. She was the ninth of eleven children. Catherine was only nine when her mother died, and in her grief she turned to Our Lady for solace. It was said that she embraced a small statue of the Blessed Virgin and stated: "Now, dear Blessed Mother, you will be my mother."

In view of the great events which were to take place later in Catherine's life, it is believed that her statement to the statue was the beginning of the Marian Age.

Catherine was a serious-minded youngster who, from the time of her first Communion, became entirely mystic. At 18 she had her first mystical experience. It came in the form of a dream. She found herself assisting at the Mass of an old priest. In her dream, he was a stranger to her, but she fled in fright. The dream continued. She went to visit a sick neighbor, and again saw the same priest. She tried to run again, but this time the priest called after her, "You do well to visit the sick, my child. You flee from me now, but one day you will be glad to come to me. God has plans for you; do not forget it."

Catherine was not to understand the significance of that dream until four years later, when she was in Paris. Actually, the village was Chatillon, near the City of Light. She was in the visitor's section Hospital of de Saint-Sauver. While she waited to visit the sick, her gaze fell on a portrait of St. Vincent de

Paul. It was the old priest in her dream!

Catherine knew then that God wanted her to become a Sister of Charity.

Catherine's First Visions

The girl of 22 entered the Sisters of Charity as a postulant at Chatillon on January 22, 1830 and spent three months there. On April 21, 1830, she entered the novitiate at 140 rue due Bac in Paris, and just in time to help at the translation of the body of St. Vincent de Paul from the Cathedral of Notre Dame to the newly erected mother church of the Vincentian Fathers. To celebrate the event, a novena of thanksgiving was held at the church.

And every night, after Catherine returned home, she was granted a vision of St. Vincent's heart.

Catherine's Visions of Jesus Christ

The young woman's novitiate lasted for nine months. According to church records, Catherine had a vision of Jesus Christ every time she looked at the Holy Eucharist. This was a constant thing and some believe that these visions lasted throughout her life.

At any rate, the vision took on a special meeting on Trinity Sunday, June 6, 1830. Christ appeared to Catherine during the Mass. He was dressed as a king in a long robe. When the Gospel was read, Catherine saw the long robe fall to the floor. She understood that to mean that the King of France, Charles X, would be overthrown. The prophecy was correct. Later in that year of 1830, a French revolution forced King Charles X to abdicate.

Catherine's Visions of Mary

Catherine was not an educated woman. Yet when she wrote of her experiences with Our Lady, she was articulate and lucid. In her own words, we now let Catherine speak:

"On the eve of the feast of St. Vincent, good Mother

Martha (Mother Superior) spoke to us of devotion to the saints and to the Blessed Virgin in particular. It gave me so great a desire to see her that I went to bed with the thought that I would see my good Mother that very night—it was a desire I had long cherished.

"We had been given a piece of a surplice of St. Vincent. I tore my piece in half, swallowed it, and fell asleep, confident that St. Vincent would obtain for me the grace of seeing the Blessed Virgin.

"At eleven-thirty, I heard someone calling my name:

"'Sister, sister, sister!'

"Wide awake, I looked in the direction of the voice. Drawing the bed-curtains, I saw a child clothed in white, some four or five years old, who said to me:

"'Come to the chapel; get up quickly and come to the chapel: the Blessed Virgin is waiting for you there.'

"At once the thought struck me: Someone will hear me.

"The child answered:

"'Do not be afraid. It is eleven-thirty; everyone is asleep. Come, I am waiting for you.'

"I followed him. He kept to my left, and was surrounded with rays of light. Wherever we went, the lights were lit, a fact which astonished me very much. But my surprise was greatest at the threshold of the chapel: the door opened of itself, the child scarcely having touched it with the tip of his finger. It was the height of everything to see that all the torches and tapers were burning—it reminded me of midnight Mass. I did not see the Blessed Virgin. The child led me into the sanctuary, to the side of the director's chair. There he remained the whole time.

"Since the time seemed long, I looked to see whether the watchers were passing by the tribunes. (Sisters on duty at night).

"Finally, the hour came; the child announced it to me, saying:

"'Here is the Blessed Virgin; here she is.'

"It would be impossible for me to describe what I felt at that moment, or what passed within me, for it seemed to me that I did now look upon the Blessed Virgin.

"It was then that the child spoke, no longer as a child, but as a grown man, and in the strangest terms.

"Looking upon the Blessed Virgin, I flung myself toward her, and falling upon my knees on the altar steps, I rested my hands in her lap.

"There a moment passed, the sweetest of my life. I could not say what I felt. The Blessed Virgin told me how I must conduct myself with my director, and added several things that I must not tell. As to what I should do in time of trouble, she pointed with her left hand to the foot of the altar, and told me to come there and to open my heart, assuring me that I would receive all the consolation that I needed.

"I asked her the meaning of everything I had seen, and she deigned to explain it to me.

"I could not say how long I stayed with her. When she left, it was as if she faded away, becoming a shadow which moved toward the tribune, the way she had come. I got up from the steps of the altar and saw that the child was where I had left him. He said:

"'She is gone...'

"We went back the same way, always surrounded with light, the child still keeping to the left.

"I believe that this child was my guardian angel, who showed himself that he might take me to see the Blessed Virgin, for I have often prayed to him to obtain this favor for me. He was dressed in white, and shone with a mysterious light that was more resplendent than the light itself; he appeared to be four or five years old."

Blessed Virgin's Prophecies to Catherine

Catherine wrote separately the statements made by the Holy Mother to her during the vision. She titled her treatise: "July Conversation With the Most Blessed Virgin, from 11:30 in the evening of the 18th until 1:30 in the morning of the 19th, St. Vincent's Day."

The Virgin Mary told her: "My child, the good God wishes to charge you with a mission. You will have much to suffer, but you will rise above these sufferings by reflecting that what you do is for the glory of God. You will know what the good God wants. You will be tormented until you have told him who is charged with directing you. You will be contradicted but, do not fear, you will have grace. Tell with confidence all that passes within you; tell it with simplicity. Have confidence, Do not be afraid.

"You will see certain things; give an account of what you see and hear. You will be inspired in your prayers; give an account of what I tell you and of what you will understand in your prayers.

"The time are very evil. Sorrows will befall France, the throne will be overturned. The whole world will be plunged into every kind of misery. But come to the foot of the altar. There graces will be shed upon all, great and small, who ask for them. Especially will graces be shed upon those who ask for them.

"My child, the cross will be treated with contempt; they will hurl it to the ground. Blood will flow, they will open up again the side of Our Lord. The streets will run with blood. Monseigneur the Archbishop will be stripped of his garments. My child, the whole world will be in sadness."

Of course, these words above are only a smattering of the two hours in which Mary spoke to Catherine. Yet a week after her appearance to the young sister, France was in turmoil. Mother Mary's predictions were correct. During the "Glorious Three Days" of the 1830 revolution in France, Archbishop de Quelen had to flee his country twice.

She also predicted that Archbishop Darboy would be executed during the revolution of 1870. He was.

Mother Mary told Catherine that during the revolution of 1848, Archbishop Affre would die. He was shot to death at the barricades.

Miracle of the Medal of the Immaculate Conception

The date of this unique miracle was November 27, 1830. The time was five-thirty in the afternoon. And it is best reported in the words of Catherine herself, who wrote them shortly after her experience.

"Several minutes after the point of the meditation I heard a sound like the rustling of a silk dress from the tribune near the picture of St. Joseph. Turning in that direction, I saw the Blessed Virgin. The Virgin was standing. She was of medium height, and clothed all in white. Her dress was of the whiteness of dawn, made in the style called 'a la Vierge,' that is, high neck and plain sleeves. A white veil covered her head and fell on either side to her feet. Under the veil her hair, in coils, was bound with a fillet, ornamented with lace. Her face was sufficiently exposed very well, and so beautiful that it seemed to me impossible to express her ravishing beauty.

"Her feet rested on a white globe, that is to say half a globe, or at least I saw only half. There was also a serpent, green in color with yellow spots.

"At this moment, while I was contemplating her, the Blessed Virgin lowered her eyes and looked at me. I heard a voice speaking these words:

"'This ball that you see represents the whole world, especially France, and each person in particular.

"I could not express what I felt at this, what I saw, the beauty and the brilliance of the dazzling rays.

"The Blessed Virgin said: 'These are the symbols of the graces I shed upon those who ask for them.'

"This made me realize how right it was to pray to the Blessed Virgin and how generous she was to those who did pray to her, what graces she gave to those who asked for them, what joy she had in giving them.

"She said: 'The gems from which rays do not fall are the graces for which souls forget to ask.'

77

"At this moment I was so overjoyed that I no longer knew where I was. A frame, slightly oval in shape, formed round the Blessed Virgin. Within it was written in letters of gold: 'O Mary, conceived without sin pray for us who have recourse to thee.'

"The inscription, in a semi-circle, began at the height of the right hand, passed over the head, and finished at the height of the left hand.

"The golden ball disappeared in the brilliance of the sheaves of light bursting from all sides; the hands turned out and the arms were bent down under the weight of the treasures of grace obtained.

"Then the voice said:

"'Have a medal struck after this model. All who wear it will receive great graces; they should wear it around the neck. Graces will abound for those who wear it with confidence.'

"At this instant the tableau seemed to me to turn, and I beheld the reverse of the Medal: a large M surmounted by a bar and a cross; beneath the M were the Hearts of Jesus and Mary, the one crowned with thorns, the other pierced with a sword."

Our Lady then vanished...

Medal Struck

Catherine had the Medal struck exactly the way she saw it. However, she was sworn to secrecy about it, and although she gave the Medal to the world, she had to remain unknown.

The Medal was Catherine's mission from God. Its correct title is the Medal of the Immaculate Conception, but the people who wore it, and saw the wonders it worked, soon changed the name to the Miraculous Medal. And eventually, Catherine Laboure did reveal how the Medal came into existence.

She died peacefully on December 31, 1876. She was beatified in 1933 by Pope Pius XI. Pope Pius XII raised her to the honor of the altar (sainthood) in 1947. Her incorrupt body still lies beneath an altar built on the spot where Our Lady appeared to her.

Miracles at La Salette

La Salette is in the French Alps and is remote, isolated, silent—or at least it was in 1846 when Our Lady appeared to two children on September 29, a Saturday afternoon.

At the time, France was in ferment. There was constant warfare and it was not confined to politics. Christianity suffered greatly in the diocese of Grenoble. There were outrageous persecutions. Very few people attended Sunday Mass. The Sacraments were neglected. Good Christians cursed more than they prayed. They indulged themselves with drinking. For a long time in that area it was as though Christianity had been crushed.

That was the atmosphere into which Mother Mary made her appearances.

The children were Melanie Mathieu, 14, and Maximin Giraud, 11. Both tended cattle but they were not really friendly with each other. Their personalities were vastly different. Melanie was morose, had no gaiety about her at all. She was timid and overdrawn. Her education was almost nil and she had no schooling in religion. She could barely recite the Lord's Prayer and the Hail Mary. But she did her job well and knew how to handle stubborn cattle.

Maximin was the exact opposite of Melanie. In his village of Corps he was regarded as a scamp. He had lots of spirit and enjoyed prowling the streets and playing games. But he, too, knew how to herd cattle.

Although they both lived in Europe, they didn't meet until

September 17. They saw each other the next day in the fields, and then on Saturday they drove their cows to a ravine to water them. While the animals drank, the two children sat down and ate some bread and cheese. After that they stretched out on the ground and took a nap.

Melanie woke first. She looked for her cows in the ravine, but her gaze was riveted to a large circle of brilliant light. It was brighter than the sun, yet it did not hurt her eyes to look at it. She called to Maximin: "Come quickly! Look at that light!"

Maximin was at her side, looking. Little by little they began to see the figure of a woman inside the light. She was seated. Her hands covered her face in an attitude of weeping.

She rose gracefully to her feet and turned to the children, her arms crossed over her breasts.

Melanie and Maximin were not bright children, but they knew now they were in the presence of something holy and supernatural.

Mary Expresses Sorrow

The children were fascinated. This lovely woman who stood before them was extremely sad. Light seemed to burst out all around her and quite distinctly were there tears on her cheeks.

She said: "Come to me, my children. Do not be afraid. I am here to tell you something of great importance."

Her French was so perfect that the children found it a little difficult to understand her. They did, however, grasp her meaning. Nevertheless, she saw their problems with her language and switched to their dialect, "If my people will not obey, I shall be compelled to loose my Son's arm. It is so heavy, so pressing that I can no longer restrain it. How long have I suffered for you! If my Son is not to cast you off, I am obliged to entreat him without ceasing. But you take no least notice of that. No matter how well you pray in the future, no matter how well you may act, you will never be able to make up to me what I have endured for your sake.

"I have appointed you six days for working. The seventh I have reserved for myself. And no one will give it to me. This it is which causes the weight of my Son's arm to be so crushing.

"The cart drivers cannot swear without bringing in my Son's name. These are the two things which make my Son's arm so burdensome.

"If the harvest is spoiled, it is your own fault. I warned you last year by means of the potatoes. You paid no heed. Quite the reverse, when you discovered that the potatoes had rotted, you swore, you abused my Son's name. They will continue to rot, and by Christmas this year there will be none left.

"If you have grain, it will do no good to sow it, for what you sow the breasts will devour, and any part of it that springs up will crumble into dust when you thresh it.

"A great famine is coming. But before that happens, the children under seven years of age will be seized with trembling and die in their parents' arms. The grownups will pay for their sins by hunger. The grapes will rot and the walnuts will turn bad."

At that point Mary spoke to Maximin, but Melanie could not hear her. She gave Maximin a secret. Then it was Melanie's turn to hear a secret that Maximin could not hear.

Then she said so that both could hear: "If people are converted, the rocks will turn to piles of wheat and it will be found that the potatoes have sown themselves." She turned away and started to leave, saying: "You will make this known to all of my people." Then she faded into the air.

The children did not know they had seen the Virgin Mary. They thought it was "some great saint." But when they told the other villagers it became clear to them that they had really seen the Holy Mother.

Unfortunately, their story was not believed by town officials and the clergy. They were subjected to an almost savage interrogation.

The Miracle of the Rock

Melanie and Maximin were grilled without let-up. The police questioned them together and separately. Priests also interrogated them. In every case it was found that the stories were exactly the same. The children never varied, never strayed from their original recital. Tricks were played on them in an effort to bring out lies. But they didn't work. Cleverly worded questions were tried, but they, too, failed. Melanie and Maximin were brought to the site where they had seen the apparition. The children showed the interrogators where the woman stood, and reported what she said. They described how she faded into the air.

The children were brought back to the site again. A policeman accused them of lying and threatened to lock them up if they didn't tell the truth. They still refused to change their story.

One man decided that it would do no harm to break off a piece of the rock the woman had sat on. He did so, and a spring of water gushed forth. This was a water source after heavy rains or when snow melted. But there had been no heavy rains for weeks. Where did the water come from? Was it a miracle? Some of the witnesses decided to find out.

The Miracle Cure

A bottle was used to capture some of the water from the spring. It was brought into town. A woman there was seriously ill. She was not expected to recover and had been ill for a long time. She was given the water. She began a novena to Our Lady and each day of it she sipped a little. By the ninth day she got out of bed and resumed her life, her health completely restored.

News of the wonderful event spread quickly. Pilgrimages began to La Salette almost overnight. First they came from nearby villages, then from more distant towns. People climbed the mountain to pray at the site of the apparition, and to gather some water from the miraculous spring—a spring that, incidentally, has never stopped flowing since that great day in September 1846.

More importantly, people returned to the church. Those who had missed Mass for years were now in regular attendance. Sundays were again used for prayer and rest. Christianity had returned to the diocese of Grenoble.

The harsh winter weather did not even slow down the people bent on making pilgrimages to La Salette. Many could not find lodging and had to spend nights in the open.

The Two Secrets

Melanie and Maximin were asked to write down the secrets that were told to them by the Holy Mother. They were reluctant to do so until they were told that only the Holy Father would see them.

The secrets were written down and placed in sealed envelopes. They were then sent to Pope Pius IX, carried to him by Father Rousselot and Father Gerin in 1851.

The secrets have never been revealed...

After nearly five years of intense investigation, Bishop de Bruillard collaborated with Bishop Villecourt of La Rochelle on a document which was sent to Rome. It was read on November 16, 1851 at every Mass in the Diocese of Grenoble. It is as follows:

"Five years ago we were told of an event most extraordinary and, at first hearing, unbelievable, as having occurred on a mountain in our diocese. It was a matter of nothing less than an apparition of the Blessed Virgin, who was said to have been seen by two herders on September 19, 1846. She told them of evils threatening her people, especially because of blasphemy and the profanation of Sunday, and she confided to each a particular secret, forbidding that these be communicated to anyone.

"In spite of the natural candor of the two herders, in spite of the impossibility of collusion by two ignorant children who hardly knew each other; in spite of the constancy and firmness of their witness, which has never varied either when confronted by the agents of the law or by thousands of persons who have exhausted every trick to involve them in contradictions or wrest the secrets from them, it has been our duty to refrain for a long time from accepting an event which seemed to us marvelous.

"While our episcopal duty imposed on us the necessity of waiting, pondering, fervently begging the light of the Holy Spirit, the numbers of wonders noised about on all sides was constantly growing. There was word of unusual cures worked in different parts of France and in other places, even countries far away. Sick people in desperate straights, either given up by their doctors as certain to die soon, or condemned to long drawn out suffering, have been reported restored to perfect health after invocation of Our Lady of La Salette and the use, with faith, of the water from the spring at which the Queen of Heaven appeared to the two herders.

"From the very first days, people have spoken to us of this spring. We have been assured that it had never before flowed steadily, but gave water only after snow or heavy rains. It was dry that September 19; thereafter it began to flow and has flowed constantly ever since: marvelous water, if not in its origin, at least in its effects."

The bishops authorized the cult of Our Lady of La Salette. In 1852, the cornerstone of the basilica was laid on the mountain where Our Lady appeared.

The shrine still draws thousands every year from all parts of the world. The number of miraculous cures continues to grow.

Just as incredible is the fact that hardened sinners who come to the shrine suddenly find themselves in a position in which they ache for a return to the church. No one has ever been able to explain it, least of all the sinners themselves, but there is a driving force which comes over them when they approach the shrine, and they are not at peace until they give themselves once again to the church they abandoned years before.

Miracles at Massabieille

An editorial in the Catholic weekly *America*, stated in part (January 1958):

"Few indeed are those who…are present as eyewitnesses of one of those rare but terribly real occurrences in which the omnipotence of God strikes through the shadows of time and space to bind up and heal the broken bodies of men. But the evidence of these visitations is indisputable. During the last century it has pleased God so to visit His people time after time at a remote grotto in the French foothills of the Pyrenees, where the Blessed Virgin Mother of God appeared in 1859 to little Bernadette Soubirous. God of course chooses His own times and places and occasions for the miraculous, but His power shines forth most frequently where His Mother is honored and venerated."

Who Was Bernadette Soubirous?

This girl of 14 was a Bigourdane peasant of sordid background. She and her family lived in abject poverty, in a hovel. In the winter months she spent most of her time trying to find wood for the fire so that her little brothers and sisters would not freeze to death. She was not especially studious, so it was not likely that she was aware of two legends that were born in her area.

One was an ancient saying that someday "a great wonder would be wrought at Massabieille." Massabieille was looked upon with disfavor. There was a grotto there where fishermen sometimes took refuge in a storm. Bernadette used it too when she was tending sheep. Despite the ancient saying, no one thought of it as a holy place.

The other legend concerned a mystic who was enraptured with a divine vision. Suddenly, the cloister bell rang, meaning he had to drop what he was doing and go to Vespers. He hesitated. What if he went to Vespers, thereby interrupting his vision? Could he return, or would the vision be lost forever?

Still his vow of obedience was important. With a great deal of reluctance, he walked away from the vision and returned to the chapel. When Vespers was over he hurried back to the sacred area and to his delight he picked up with the vision at the exact point he had left off. He heard a Divine Voice say: "If you had not done your manifest duty, your vision would have vanished and you would never have known its culmination. What is me, you would never have another."

Bernadette was probably not aware of the legend, but it does strike a similar note in her own case: If she had not gone for wood at the grotto, she would not have seen the Beautiful Lady who changed the lives of millions.

Bernadette's Vision at Lourdes

J.B. Estrade was a close friend of Bernadette's. He was a minor government official who took the time and effort to record the girl's statement word for word regarding her divine experience. This is her story:

"The Thursday before Ash Wednesday (February 11, 1858), it was cold and the weather was threatening. After our dinner my mother told us that there was no more wood in the house and she was vexed. My sister Toinette and I, to please her, offered to go and pick up dry branches by the riverside. My mother said 'no' because the weather was bad and we might be in danger of falling into the Gave. Jeanne Abadie, our neighbor, wanted to come with us. My mother still hesitated, but seeing that there were three of us, she let us go. As soon as we reached the end of a field, nearly opposite the grotto of

Massabieille, we were stopped by the canal of a mill we had just passed. The current of this canal was not strong for the mill was not working, but the water was cold and I for my part was afraid to go in. Jeanne Abadie and my sister, less timid than I, took their sabots (shoes) in their hand and crossed the stream. However, when they were on the other side, they called out that it was cold and bent down to rub their feet and warm them. All this increased my fear, and I thought that if I went into the water I should get an attack of asthma. So I asked Jeanne, who was bigger and stronger than I, to take me on her shoulders.

"'I should think not,' she answered. 'You're a mollycoddle; if you won't come, stay where you are.'"

"After the others had picked up some pieces of wood under the grotto they disappeared along the Gave. When I was alone I threw stones into the bed of the river to give me a foothold. But it was of no use. So I had to make up my mind to take off my sabots and cross the canal as Jeanne and my sister had done.

"I had just begun to take off my first stocking when suddenly I heard a great noise like the sound of a storm. I looked to the right, to the left, under the trees of the river, but nothing moved; I thought I was mistaken. I went on taking off my shoes and stockings; then I heard a fresh noise like the first. I was frightened and stood straight up. I lost all power of speech and thought when, turning my head toward the grotto, I saw at once of the openings of the rock a rosebush, one only, moving as if it were very windy. Almost at the same time there came out of the interior of the grotto a golden-colored cloud, and soon after a Lady, young and beautiful, exceedingly beautiful, the like of whom I had never seen, came and placed herself at the entrance of the opening above the rosebush. She looked at me immediately, smiled at me, and signalled to me to advance, as if she had been my mother. All fear had left me but I seemed to know no longer where I was. I rubbed my eyes, I shut them,

I opened them; but the Lady was still there continuing to smile at me and making me understand that I was not mistaken. Without thinking of what I was doing, I took my rosary in my hands and went on my knees. The Lady made a sign of approval with her head and herself took into her hands a rosary which hung on her right arm. When I attempted to begin the rosary and tried to lift my hand to my forehead, my arm remained paralyzed, and it was only after the Lady had made the sign of the cross. that I could do the same. The Lady left me to pray all alone; she passed the beads of the rosary between her fingers but she said nothing; only at the end of each decade did she say the 'Glorida' with me.

"When the recitation of the rosary was finished, the Lady returned to the interior of the rock and the golden cloud disappeared with her."

Miracle of Warm Water

Bernadette continues, noting the temperature of the canal water:

"As soon as the Lady disappeared Jeanne and my sister returned to the grotto and found me on my knees in the same place where they had left me. They laughed at me, called me an imbecile and bigot, and asked me if I would go back with them or not. I had now no difficulty in going into the stream, and I felt the water as warm as the water for washing dishes.

"'You had no reason to make an outcry,' I said to Jeanne and Toinette while drying my feet, 'the water of the canal is not so cold as you seemed to make me believe.'

"'You are very fortunate not to find it so; we found it very cold.'"

Bernadette told the other two about her vision. The girls believed her; her mother did not. In fact, when Bernadette wanted to go back to the grotto, her mother refused permission. After three days of begging, the mother threw up her hands and let her daughter go.

On the second vision, Bernadette was accompanied only by her friends, who saw nothing. On the third visit, many of the townspeople came along, too. One of them brought a blessed candle. Mother Mary told Bernadette that she was to come to the grotto fifteen times at regular intervals. No reason was given for this command, but the Virgin Mary did tell the girl that she would not be happy in this world, and that happiness awaited her in heaven.

Fifth Visit and the Mysterious Prayer

On this visit Mary taught Bernadette a prayer which she recited as long as she lived. However, the girl never revealed the words to anyone. Mary also asked the girl to bring a blessed candle on her next visit, which Bernadette did. Today, candles burn perpetually at the shrine.

Eighth Vision and the Puzzling Request

Mother Mary's strong words to Bernadette were always the same: "Penitence! Penitence! Penitence!" She repeated them during the eighth visit, and this time Mary told the girl, "Drink from the fountain and bathe in it!"

Bernadette was puzzled. There was no fountain at Massabieille; there never had been. The girl then dropped to her knees and began to scratch the earth. Soon moisture appeared. Then a small puddle. Bernadette cupped the water and drank it. Later, she washed her face. The next day the pool was overflowing and dripped down over the rocks. The following day there was a stream which has never stopped flowing.

Skeptics insist the water was there all along. But how did Bernadette know where to dig? The answer is that she knew because she was given a direct command.

The Miracle of Fire

On one occasion, Bernadette knelt at the grotto and

prayed while the Holy Mother looked on. The girl held a candle in her left hand. Her right hand moved outward, away from her body, and directly into the flame of another candle. Behind her there were cries of horror as the onlookers saw what was happening. Still, Bernadette did not move her right hand away from the flame; she held it there for fifteen minutes. Spectators could see the flame gleaming through her fingers.

When the vision faded, Bernadette's hand was examined. It was not even singed! A wag nearby thrust a lighted candle at her hand. Bernadette gasped in pain and cried out, "You are burning me!"

Our Lady of Lourdes

Bernadette's visions of the Holy Mother lasted from February to July. Miracles were performed, of course—the miracle of warm water and the miracle of fire. But there were no great prophecies here. Mary's only message at the grotto concerned the miraculous healing powers of the water she created out of dry and barren ground.

The records show that the healings include mental as well as physical. Lourdes has become perhaps the leading shrine for the halt, the lame and the blind from all parts of the world. The condition of every sufferer going to Lourdes must be certified by his parish priest and his personal physician.

There is an official board that passes on cures and is made of Catholics, non-Catholics and even non-Christians. They are unimpeachable doctors of many nationalities. It is therefore impossible for a false claim to get by these people.

Statue of Our Lady of Fatima Moves!

The vision of the Holy Mother appeared to Lucy, Jacinta and Francisco on the 13th of every month for six months. But that was in 1917. Today, the Virgin still makes her presence known on the 13th of every month. It's not at Fatima, but at the Mater Ecclesiae Catholic Church in Thornton, California.

In that church there is a statue of Our Lady of Fatima. It is four feet tall and weighs 60 pounds. On the 13th of every month since 1981 it has moved by forces that can only be described as supernatural.

A church volunteer, Albert Amaro, says: "We keep finding her at the altar. My wife saw her cry."

There are six people who have keys to the church. Each suspected the other of playing games. That problem was solved one night when the church was locked and the statue was bolted to a stand. A few days later, on the 13th of that month, the statue was found 20 feet away from its original position.

Bishop Roger M. Mahoney has appointed a committee to investigate the matter.

Many call the moving and weeping statue a miracle. We can also assume that Mother Mary was aware of the church's plight and did something about it. Until the moving statue episode, Mater Ecclesiae Catholic Church had not been doing well financially. Now, attendance at Sunday Mass has tripled. On the 13th of every month more than 1,000 people flock to the church. Thousands so far have spent two dollars each to light a candle at the statue, and enough money has been collected by the church to have its roof remodeled with a skylight, a project that cost $16,000.

Strange Light on Film

One of those who came to light a candle at the statue of Our Lady of Fatima was a woman named Joyce Davis. Ms. Davis is not Catholic. Still, she was drawn to the little mission church in Thornton, and she lit a candle with the hope that the flame would unite with the many thousands being lit and offered around the world. To Ms. Davis, the candle represented hearts aflame with praise and thanksgiving that we in this country are allowed the privilege of assembly for the purpose of showing our gratitude for the gift of life.

The woman was quite moved by the recitation of the rosary. She was also awed by the floral offerings, the statue itself, and the feeling that a Divine Presence was near.

Ms. Davis' only thought now was to capture the moment on film. She approached the statue of Our Lady of Fatima and snapped a picture.

The date was December 19, 1982.

When the woman had the film processed she was amazed to see that in the upper left corner of the picture was a brilliant globe of red and white light surrounded by a fiery aura.

She did not see such a light in the church when she took the picture. She returned to the church to make sure there was no light in the background behind the statue. There was no light. The woman talked to photographers, showed them the photo. They had no explanation. She talked to church officials. They could not give her an answer, but she does feel that she has one.

Ms. Davis said: "I feel that you have given me a very special answer to the petition that I placed before you on December 19, 1982, just a short time before the entire world joined in the annual celebration of the anniversary of the birth of your Beloved Son, Jesus. And, though the skeptics may render a different opinion, I shall hold this thought in my mind and my heart and treasure it always."

Ms. Davis' petition was a simple one: "Beloved Lady, how I long for the day when this kind of Unity will be the prevailing factor upon this planet, replacing the divisions which now persist among the children of Earth.

"How I long to hear the Earth resounding with Songs of Praise instead of the constant tumult that presently exists."

The strange light on Ms. Davis' photo has still not been explained.

More likely, it's living proof that Mother Mary works in mysterious ways. It should also be remembered that several times recently she had indicated that her presence would be made known on photographic film as has been the case in the visions in Bayside, Queens and elsewhere.

Our Lady of Knock

The apparitions at Knock, Ireland, on August 21, 1879, were almost entirely different from all other apparitions recorded. We list the differences here:

1. Our Lady made no statement, did not admonish and did not prophesy.

2. Our Lady did not acknowledge the presence of those who saw her.

3. Our Lady was accompanied by St. Joseph and St. John. Angels were present. There was an altar and a sacrificial lamb on the altar.

4. The privilege of seeing Our Lady was not confined to children. She was seen by 18 people, including three men, two children, two teenage boys and a girl, and six women. The other four individuals, men and women, reported seeing a great light covering the whole gable of the church where the visions occurred.

5. Our Lady's standing position, arms raised to the heavens, eyes upward, was never duplicated in Marian art. All of the statues in her likeness show her with her arms at her sides or crossed in front of her. To find a piece of art showing her with arms upraised, one would have to return to the ancient Christians and their primitive work. This would indicate that the 18 people who saw Our Lady were not influenced by statues.

Why Mary Came to Knock

Knock was a remote village in the west of Ireland, a place of forgotten fields and forlorn houses. Its county, Mayo, in 1879, was one of the hardest hit financially. The people were desperately poor. Many of them lived under the thumbs of rack-renting landlords who didn't even live in Ireland. These suffering people were at the mercy of grasping agents, evictions, emigrations, recurring famines and fevers, general misery and desolation.

As we know, conditions like these usually tear at the Immaculate Heart of the Holy Mother, especially when the sufferers keep the faith despite their poverty. Mary came to Knock to alleviate the terrible pain of her children.

The Knock church was dedicated to St. John the Baptist and it was so small that it held only thirty people. There was a statue of Our Lady, one of St. Joseph and one of St. Aloysius. A few small windows let in light.

It was outside this little church that the apparitions occurred.

The Knock Apparitions

Heavy rains fell on August 21, 1879. The storm lasted all day and far into the night. It was as though Satan was trying to discourage people from walking outside because he knew Mary was about to make an appearance.

But he failed. Villagers had to conduct business, go on errands, and shop. Two women were on their way to visit a dying friend when they saw a great light near the cement wall surrounding the Knock church. They saw three figures in the light and their immediate reactions were that the archdeacon just had delivery of three new statues for the church. The first three had been destroyed in a storm a year earlier. But they wondered why the priest had left the statues out in the rain.

The women moved closer. The figures were actually at the gable wall of the church...and they were moving! One of the women cried, "They're not statues! It's the Blessed Virgin!"

The three visions were not standing on the ground, but on

top of the tall grass and about a foot from the wall itself. The central figure was Our Lady. On her right, and lower in height, was St. Joseph. He appeared old and had a long gray beard. On her left, and lower, was St. John the Evangelist. He wore a small mitre. Statues of St. John always show him bare-headed.

One of the women rushed home to tell her family. When they returned, the other women left to tell hers. Eventually, 14 people stood in the teeming rain to look at the wonderful visions.

They stood there, praying and taking in the details. They saw a brilliant golden light. Three figures moved in front of a large cross on an altar which was higher than the figures. A young lamb stood facing west. Angels hovered above. Their wings could be heard fluttering, but no one saw their faces because they were turned to the three figures. The angels were seen for about an hour and a half.

Mary's arms were raised and in the same position as a priest's when he prays at Mass. Her gaze was fixed on the sky and she did not look at any time at the people watching her.

A woman named Bridget Trench, on her knees, exclaimed, "A hundred thousand thanks to God and to the Glorious Virgin for showing us this sight." She was so entranced that she went to the gable in an effort to embrace the Holy Mother's feet. But her arms closed on empty air.

Bridget said later, "I felt nothing in the embrace but the wall, yet the figures appeared so full and so lifelike and so lifesize that I could not understand it and wondered why my hands could not feel what was so plain and distinct to my sight."

Bridget Trench remarked how heavily the rain fell that night, and said: "I felt the ground carefully with my hands and it was perfectly dry. The wind was blowing from the south, right against the gable, but no rain fell on that portion of the gable where the figures were."

By a quarter after eleven that evening the apparitions finally faded from view.

The Miracles at Knock

Local and national newspapers in Ireland were requested by the clergy not to report the happenings at Knock. But that edict did not stop the people from talking about it. So the news spread quickly by word of mouth. Four months later, when newspapers did mention the story, everyone in the Catholic world knew about it.

The miracles began about ten days after the great event. A deaf child was cured. A man who was born blind was able to see after he made a pilgrimage to Knock. Another man was so close to death that he had to be carried to Knock. He vomited blood most of the way. Then the deathly ill man drank some water in which a scrap of cement from the gable had been dissolved. He was instantly cured!

In no time at all seven or eight cures a week were being reported, among them cases of paralysis, blindness, epilepsy, cancer, heart trouble, bone disease, and tuberculosis. It was learned that many of these cures had taken place because the sick and dying had taken water with some of the cement from the gable in it.

As expected, people began to chip away at the cement wall for sick friends at home or overseas. The crowds at the Knock church were tremendous and the gable gave signs of having a severe weakness. Nevertheless, a nun in Arabia wrote the archdeacon that a piece of the cement from the gable had saved a young Sister from a wasting disease. A mother in Autun, France was cured of cancer, a Michigan woman of dropsy and a Newfoundland carpenter of a serious hand injury.

Invalids came to Knock from every county in Ireland. Some of them walked 200 miles or more. One elderly man had a large, ugly growth on his neck that reached down to his chest. He was so weak that he had to walk with a stick and use a young boy to lean on. He left County Limerick. Children stared in horror at his deformity. Adults merely shook their heads, saying that he was so old it was not likely he'd ever

98

make it to Knock.

Several weeks later, however, the villagers at Limerick were astounded when the man returned. The growth was gone. He was well and strong. A close-up inspection of his neck showed that it was completely cured.

When he was asked what had happened, he said the cure came suddenly, while he was making a "Station." What he meant was that he made the "Stations of the Cross" at Knock.

Witness describes to police and reporters how the apparition of the Virgin Mary came in a ball of light to her backyard. The woman has put up a shrine at the spot where she saw the vision.

Incredible Happenings at San Damiano

The same Italian village at San Damiano is located in the Emilie and Lombardie provinces. It is 15 kilometers south of Piacenza and 70 kilometers southeast of Milan.

The Holy Mother has been appearing in this village every Friday at noon since October 16, 1964. She also appears on every feast day of Jesus and Mary, and on every day in May, and always at the same hour. Only one person can see and hear Mary. She is Rosa Quattrini.

Rosa Quattrini is a simple peasant, ignorant of world affairs. However, she is known everywhere for her sincerity, charity, courage and piety. Rosa was born on January 26, 1909 and has led a life of great suffering and continual sickness.

The woman married on October 7, 1937 and spent her married life devoted to her husband. She worked hard despite her illnesses, and had always known poverty.

Mother Mary selected Rosa as her link with the world.

Rosa's Miraculous Cure

Rosa had three children, all by caesarean operations. All were extremely painful. The operations were not successful because the wounds did not heal. There were five wounds. Complications set in. The woman suffered peritonitis, infection, stubborn high fevers and anemia. Her reproductive organs were actually mutilated.

After the birth of her last child, Rosa spent most of her time in hospitals. Every treatment known to medical science was tried on her. Finally, her situation became so desperate that the hospital sent her home to die.

The date was September 29, 1961, the Feast of St. Michael the Archangel. Rosa took to her bed on the first floor of her house and suffered greatly. The following account of her miraculous cure is taken from a book on San Damiano by Jean-Gabriel. In it, you will see references to Padre Pio, the famed priest who was a stigmatic for 50 years. Rosa and Padre Pio had sixteen meetings before his death. The account of the miracle follows:

"I was lying in bed and I couldn't move. My husband had gone to look for chestnuts. Only my Aunt Adele was home. It was a hot day.

A young woman came around noontime and asked for an offering. She wanted to light three candles, three little lamps in the Sanctuary of Our Lady of Grace at San Giovanni where Padre Pio was. It would cost 500 lire.

Aunt Adele said, "But we are very poor. Between us, we have 1,000 lire (about $1.50 in American money) at home and even this was borrowed."

The lady said, "Nevertheless, you should make the offering."

"I have always given offerings,' said Aunt Adele, "but today we really cannot. My niece, Rosa, is there, suffering the pains of hell; she must be taken care of and we have only these 1,000 lire."

"Where is your niece?" asked the lady.

"She is there," answered Aunt Adele.

Then the lady came in and saw me lying in bed.

"Come, courage! What is the matter with you?"

"I am all torn open," I answered.

"Give me your hand," she said.

I gave her my hand, but it was useless.

Then she said to me., "Give me both your hands."

I gave her both my hands and felt a great shock.

"Come, get up!" she told me again.

I got up. I was cured!

I began to shout, "I'm cured! I'm cured!"

But she said to me, "Be quiet!" She then directed me to recite the Angelus and five Our Fathers, five Hail Marys and five Glorias for Padre Pio's intentions.

I recited them and then she placed her hands on my wounds, and the wounds were healed instantly.

Rosa was asked what this lady looked like. "Her face was very beautiful," she said. "She was dressed as a peasant. She told me that she came from very far away. She then told Rosa, "You must go to Padre Pio."

"With what money?" I asked. "The landlord has taken everything."

"You must not stay here," she said. "Find another house. Then you must go to Padre Pio."

"But I have no money, none for either food or clothing for the trip."

"Do not think about it," she replied. "At the proper moment, you will have all that is necessary."

A short time later Rosa received a letter containing enough money for the trip. There was no return address on the envelope. Two hours before her journey, two dresses arrived. They fit perfectly, but no one knew who sent them.

But on that day of the miracle, Aunt Adele gave the beautiful lady 500 lire. Then the young woman went away. Rosa's little boy, playing outside, saw her leave. There were other people there, but only the boy saw her.

Rosa went to San Giovanni Rotondo and saw the woman again. "Do you recognize me?" she asked. "Make it known that I am the Mother of Consolation and of the Afflicted. After Holy Mass I will conduct you to Padre Pio who will give you a mission to accomplish."

Rosa's Mission

Rosa told Padre Pio about the miracle and about the meeting with the Holy Mother. The saintly priest responded: "Return home, take care of the sick."

Rosa did exactly that for two and a half years. She tended the sick in hospitals and in their homes. When her Aunt Adele became ill with bronchitis, Padre Pio told Rosa to devote all of her time to her aunt.

It was Rosa's practice to pray to the Madonna every night. On one occasion, the Madonna told her that one day she would see the field between her house and the road filled with little houses. The prediction came true. Years later the little houses were actually house trailers owned by the pilgrims to San Damiano!

Rosa was in her kitchen one day when a priest entered. He was about 30. He asked if he might pray with her. She agreed.

Rosa was stuck by the man's beautiful prayers. She was eager to learn the words in order to praise the Lord. The priest told her to say the rosary. "It is beautiful and powerful," he said. "The more simple your prayer, the more it will please God."

Rosa asked the priest where he was from and he replied, "I am a Nazarene." The woman did not understand the word, but said: "Come to see me again." Her back was to the priest. When she turned to face him he was gone.

During her conversation with the priest she told him that she had completely forgotten the Mysteries of the Rosary. Now, alone in he kitchen, she said the rosary and felt her head being held by two invisible hands. She heard a voice repeat the Mysteries of the Rosary seven times. Since then, she has never forgotten them.

Days later, the Madonna told her that the young priest was Jesus of Nazareth.

Rosa's First Apparition

The pear tree in Rosa Quattrini's garden was the focal

point of the apparition which took place on October 16, 1964, at noon. Her account of this event follows:

"On October 16, 1964, at noontime I was here; I was reciting the Angelus. I was right at this table and I was praying when I heard a voice outside calling me: 'Come! Come forward! Come, I am waiting for you!' I went out and saw a big white cloud in the sky with many golden and silver stars and many roses of all colors. A globe came out of the cloud, a red globe, which descended to the pear tree.

"Then, the Heavenly Mama came out of the globe, clothed in great light. She had a great Mantle and a crown of stars and above Her head, a great light. She said to me:

"'My little girl, I come from far away. Announce to the world that all must pray because Jesus can no longer carry the cross. I want all to be saved: the good and the wicked. I am the Mother of Love, the Mother of all; you are all My children. That is why I want all to be saved. That is why I have come; to bring the world to prayer because the chastisements are near. I will return each Friday and I will give you messages and you must make them known to the world.'

"Then I said to Her, 'But how will they believe me? I am only a poor, ignorant peasant. I have no authority. They'll throw me in prison!' She replied, 'Do not fear, because now I will leave you a sign. You will see it: this tree will blossom!'"

The Miracle of the Pear Tree

That same day the entire tree blossomed despite the fact that the month was October and pears are out of season. The tree almost immediately became covered with flowers while still laden with fruit. Close to the pear tree was a plum tree, and that part of the plum tree that was touched by the Madonna was also covered with white flowers. The tree was photographed in bloom and written up in local newspapers.

People the world over have been coming to San Damiano ever since the first apparition. Pilgrims spend their days and nights in prayer at the little garden holding the pear tree. Rosa comes to that spot every Friday at noon. Those who stand near her turn on tape recorders to catch every word she utters. The woman raises her eyes to the apparition and keeps them there for the entire period. She asks questions of the "Mamma," and repeats the answers aloud so that they may be recorded.

Witnesses say that there is no way Rosa could possibly memorize the answers because, apparently, she does not have the mental capacity to do so. Too, the speech pattern is entirely different. Rosa's sentence structure is far different from the structure of the answers she received. Rosa always begins the session by saying, "The Heavenly Mamma is present."

Rosa is sometimes weary, and it shows. For years and years she has been reciting the rosary at the pear tree, during intense heat and biting cold.

Mother Mary has given thousands of messages through Rosa at San Damiano, but there are five principal events which stand out. All of them are concerned with the future. They are: the Coming of San Damiano; the Chastisements; the Great Light which will be given in the world; the triumph of Mary; the new reign of Jesus.

The Coming of San Damiano

Mary said on August 8, 1966: "Here I want a great Sanctuary. I want all my children. This Sanctuary must have fifteen altars in honor of the fifteen Mysteries of the Rosary. One day this place will rise triumphant. A day will come when the bells of San Damiano will ring in celebration. The whole world will come here at my feet, from all nations. I want an International Center of the entire world. All will come and prostrate themselves in prayer. I promised this to my instrument (Rosa) the first day I came. I announced that the whole world would come here at my feet, that I want an International Center of the entire world under the title of 'Roses,' the greatest Sanctuary in the world."

The Chastisements

On December 1, 1967, Mary asked: "Do you not see the chastisements occurring in all parts of the world?"

This is a recurring theme with the Holy Mother. She does not spell out what the chastisements will be, perhaps because they are so awesome. However, she does warn:

"Jesus is merciful. he waits. He waits to see what you do. But afterwards, chastisements will pounce heavily upon humanity: chastisements of all kinds! Why do you not listen to your Heavenly Mamma who loves you so?

"Do you not see the world is rushing forward into the abyss and destruction? I have been announcing these chastisements to you for a long time. The Eternal Father is weary. When you see the fire and the whole world burning, what will become of you who do not listen to the maternal word? When this terrible chastisement comes, what will become of them if they are not believed?

"I have suffered so with love and sorrow to save humanity! And now, to see it going to perdition. You do not understand the sacrifice I made along the Sorrowful Way of Calvary: step by step, to follow my Son, crucified, to save all humanity. But few understand the shout of a Mother who remains terrified."

The Holy Mother added: "The Eternal Father is the Father of Love. He is merciful. But, now, He has said, 'Enough! My children. Enough! Because you do not listen to My Spouse: A Mother who weeps, who shouts for help to save her sons!'"

The Great Light

In 1968, Mother Mary made an astonishing announcement. We present it here in its entirety:

"Soon, I will come, my children! Soon, I will be in your midst with a great light. I will enlighten the entire world. Many souls will cry because they did not listen to my call.

"Blessed are those who believe and hope in me! For when I come with the light, I will place much joy in their hearts; never before will they have experienced all the love I give to my sons.

"But for those who insult me, those who do not believe, the Eternal Father will place such anguish in their hearts, such remorse and so many tears, that they will no longer have peace.

"You will see one day: you will see a great light in the sky which will pass everywhere. I will pass above everyone in a cloud and everyone will see me. What will become of those who insulted me and made a laughing stock of me? My poor sons, what will their conscience be when they present themselves before the Tribunal of God?

"I will come soon, my sons, to travel through the entire world. I will give a great sign in the sky for those who will still want to be saved. All those who have recourse to me, who have a look of repentance, this will be sufficient to save them.

"I will come soon with a great light to convert many souls. And then, the heavens and the earth will tremble by my power. Then all minds will be enlightened and all hearts will be set on fire with love for me."

The Triumph of Mary

The triumph of Mary can be found in the Apocalypse. Several prophets have also mentioned it. Mother Mary spoke of it at San Damiano. She spoke of it at Fatima, saying that the triumph would be that of her Sorrowful and Immaculate Heart. It will be a triumph of love. It will cause Hell to tremble and the elect to rejoice. It will be the triumph, finally, of good over evil.

Mary said at San Damiano in 1968: "I will soon come in great triumph. I will awaken hearts. I will pardon all who ask, who hope, who love.

"I will come in my power, and I will open the heavens, the clouds. I will enlighten the whole world. Many souls will be converted and many souls will enter into Heaven. A great, great number will leave this earth. Prepare yourselves, my children, for the hour approaches! If you have Jesus in your heart, Jesus will give you the strength, Jesus will give you the courage to arrive into glory."

The day will be great, but also quite fearsome. The indication is that a great many will die ("leave the earth") and others will find great joy in Mary's triumph. The suggestion that Hell will tremble tells us that Satan will be defeated. The final blow for Satan, however, will come with the new reign of Jesus.

The New Reign of Jesus

On December 29, 1967, Mother Mary told Rosa: "Jesus will return on this earth. His reign will be one of mercy and pardon for all. Jesus will come with a great procession of angels, and martyrs. He will go on all roads everywhere."

There was much more. The Virgin Mary revealed great things concerning the new reign of Jesus when she spoke to Rosa at San Damiano. It was an extraordinary message, and we repeat it here:

"The Father has given power to the daughter to fulfill her mission as mother towards her children. He gives her power, He gives her help. He gives her strength and knowledge to accomplish all that the Mother of God asks for her sons because she wants to protect and save them with her very great love of Merciful Mother.

"The Father, the Son and the Holy Spirit permit the Mother of all to walk the earth because she wants to save her sons. She loves them with so great a love.

"The Eternal Father has given all power to His Spouse (the Most Blessed Virgin) to accomplish a great mission on this earth and to prepare all her sons with a pure heart, full of love, recognition, and affection towards their Heavenly Mamma, and to enflame all hearts for the coming of the Universal King upon the Earth.

"The reign of Jesus will pour an ardent fraternal love into the hearts of her sons and will exterminate all the heresies, sin, all evil, and will throw all the demons back into the depths of the abyss.

"All those who remain will have a great light and will accomplish something great, something very, very great on this earth!

"Jesus will pass along the roads of the world with His Apostles, with the Saints and with the Angels, with all the Heavenly court, with a perfume of love, of great goodness and tenderness for all.

"Jesus and Mary will always be with you, in the heavens, on the earth, on the ocean, together everywhere, in great joy and triumph with me.

"And this bright star will enlighten the whole world with great joy for all those who will have suffered, endured, for my love.

"Suffer! Suffer with me because your Mamma of Heaven suffers so for her sons: especially for my sons of predilection who have forsaken me and my Son, Jesus, in great anguish. They are true apostles and now they have allowed themselves to be monopolized by diabolical temptation and they commit so many errors, so many sacrileges! But I still have mercy for them.

"Unite yourselves, my sons! Unite yourselves, you who are here in my presence. Pray, so that they may take the arm of a loving Mother, Mother of the sons that I love so. That they may save themselves and also all the sons that Jesus has confided to them."

Mary Tells of a Terrible Battle to Come

"Reign of Jesus! Reign of Mary! In the entire world, in all hearts, with great joy and love! Confide in me, hope in me, and remain serene! Rest upon my Heart and do not allow yourself to be tempted, because the hour is coming. The Devil stands fast with ferocity in the great terrible combat. He will not conquer because my power will crush his head. Do not lose courage, my sons! Increase always in faith!

"But when this day comes when Heaven and earth will open, it will be a terrible battle of anguish and tears. Thunder and lightning will make a great din! But you, do not fear. Recite many Credos. Pray very much to St. Michael the Archangel with the rosary in your hands, that he give you strength, courage in the great battle. And you will be safe on the earth and will win eternal happiness in Heaven."

Mary Offers Wonders

"But when this calamity will be terminated and you see Heaven opened, it will be an immense joy for you, and you will never be able to comprehend the beauty, the grandeur, the goodness and the mercy of God.

"Listen to me, my sons, listen to your Mamma of Heaven who does everything for you! I left my Son, Jesus, in Heaven to come here and save you, to give you a great grace and celestial blessing! Prepare yourselves, my children! Prepare yourselves with a heart gentle and serene, in this month, and do not be troubled for I am close to you, I, with your Guardian Angel, with St. Michael the Archangel, with your Patron Saint. We will assist you minute by minute. Do not be troubled.

"Pray! Pray! Pray! Always with a smile on your lips."

Mary's Promises

"Those who must leave this earth will arrive in Heaven with a great company of Angels and will, return on the earth to comfort, to pray, to console all their brothers.

"Listen to me, my children! Listen to me! It is I who am speaking to you! I am your Mamma, the Queen of the Rosary, Miraculous Mamma, Mamma of Grace and Pardon. Put my words into practice and reflect!

"Pray more, day after day, and you will have the strength to plod on with the Cross on your shoulders up to Calvary where Jesus awaits you. There, you will find my son, Jesus, risen, at His Sepulcher. You will also rise to a new life of sanctity with the Angels and with the Saints.

"I bless all those present and all those who will come to surround me and listen to my invitation. I bless you and I pour graces and blessings upon you."

These prophecies and blessings were spoken by Mother Mary to Rosa Quattrini on November 22, 1967. It is interesting to note that Jesus confirmed Mary's warning about the end of time when He told Rosa on December 15, 1967: "I, Myself will come on this earth with many Angels, many Saints, many Patriarchs, many Prophets, and all of the Apostles."

A woman of simple means, Rosa's visions have brought thousands to the tiny town in which she lives. The above photo was taken at San Samiano, Italy on Nov. 27, 1971. It shows Our Lady standing above the sun in a very clear and dramatic photo. The miracle was witnessed by 15,000 pilgrims.

Visions At Zeitoun

One of the more recent—very well documented—visions occurred in Zeitoun, which is a poor suburb of Cairo, Egypt. This one began on April 2, 1968 and lasted well over three years.

The population of Cairo is mostly Moslem, but there is a fairly large Coptic Catholic minority in the city and it boasts of having a beautiful church known as St. Mary's Church of Zeitoun.

Actually, the vision occurred first on April 2nd and 3rd. At the time, two mechanics were working in a city garage across the street from the church, which stands at Tomanbey Street and Khalil Lane. The mechanics happened to look over at the church and were startled to see a nun dressed in white standing on top of the large dome at the center of the roof and holding onto the stone cross at the top of the dome.

Their first reaction was that the nun was about to commit suicide by jumping to the ground. One of the men ran into the church to get a priest while the other telephoned for an emergency squad.

The priest was the first to recognize the event for what it was—a Marian vision. The figure remained in view for a few minutes, then disappeared. The news of Mary's visit spread rapidly, and crowds formed around the church to see the miracle. But the Virgin Mary did not make an appearance again until April 9th, a Tuesday. Nevertheless, crowds of people saw her standing atop the dome of the church and were awed.

Fortunately, an American priest named Rev. J. Palmer rushed to Zeitoun as soon as he heard about the phenomenon and was able to investigate it first hand.

He learned, for instance, that in the early 1920s the Khalil Family donated the land that St. Mary's Church of Zietoun stands on. At the time, a revelation was made to one of the family members that the Mother of God would appear in the church for one year.

Rev. Palmer saw the apparition and tells us: "The apparitions of Our Lady are usually heralded by mysterious lights. Not only does the Blessed Mother appear in a burst of brilliant light, so bright the spectators find it impossible in most cases to distinguish features, but flashing scintillating lights, compared by witnesses to flourescent lights or sheet lightning, precede the appearances by approximately a quarter of an hour. These sheflas appear sometimes above the church, sometimes in the clouds that on occasion form over the church and cover it like a canopy."

Rev. Palmer also talks about the mysterious clouds which accompany the apparition: "One should include perhaps the 'lights'—the mysterious clouds that are sometimes seen hovering over the church, even when the rest of the sky was cloudless. One night, Bishop Gregorius stated, there poured from the sealed, stained-glass windows of the high dome, such clouds of incense that it would take millions of sensors to produce a like quantity. The incense cloud settled over the throng standing around the church.

"Another phenomenon witnessed by the spectators is the appearance of bird-like creatures before, during and after the apparitions, and sometimes on nights when there is no apparition at all. These creatures in some ways resemble doves. They are larger than doves, they are larger even than pigeons. Whence they come or whither they go no one can determine. It is known, says the keeper of the Cairo zoo, that pigeons do not fly at night. But these can hardly be any kind of natural bird.

"First of all, the birds fly too rapidly. They fly without ever moving their wings. They seem to glide before, into and around the apparition. They never came to rest on the roof or trees, and on some occasions have been seen to disintegrate in the sky like wisps of clouds."

Rev. Palmer described the birds as being spotless white, and emitting light. He said they were electrically illuminated birds which could be seen in the brilliance of the apparition and also in the darkness of the sky above the vision. They appeared and disappeared without any sound at all.

In Rev. Palmer's work, *Our Lady Returns to Egypt,* he documents the various attitudes of the Blessed Mother. "At first, she appeared above the dome of the church in traditional form, wearing the veil and long robes associated with other appearances, such as at Lourdes and Fatima. There is nothing perceptible other than light, and that is described by Bishop Athanasius as bluish white or whitish blue. It is somewhat like the color of the sky on a clear day.

"Mary does not stand motionless, but is seen blowing and greeting the people in silence. She bends from the waist, moves her arms in greeting and blessing and sometimes holds out an olive branch to the people.

"She has appeared between the trees in the courtyard in front of the church; she has appeared under each of the four small domes, through the windows of the larger dome, and has often walked about on the flat church roof so as to be seen by those standing on all sides of the church."

The duration of the apparitions varied greatly. They lasted from a few minutes to several hours. On the night of June 8, 1968 they remained visible from 9:00 p.m. to 4:30 a.m. The visions of the Blessed Mother continued from 1968 through 1970, and many photographs were taken, a few of which are reproduced along with this text.

Mary Remained Silent

Although there were a great many cures at Zeitoun, the

Blessed Mother elected not to speak from her lofty perch atop the church. There were no warnings or admonitions from her this time. There was no individual recipient to whom she could communicate her thoughts. It was obvious that in Zeitoun she hoped to reach as many people as possible by appearing at the church for a period of three years.

The important difference here, as opposed to the visions at Fatima, is that the Virgin Mary made herself visible to thousands of people, believers and nonbelievers. At Fatima, only the three children were granted the distinction of seeing Mary.

Vision at Sabana Grande

The date was April 23, 1953. The locale: Rincon de Sabana Grande, Puerto Rico. The witnesses: Juan Angel Collado and two sisters, Ramonita and Isidra Belen.

The children said that not far from their elementary school there is a small spring under some mango trees. It was at the spring, they insist they saw the Virgin Mary.

At first, most of the people discredited the story as childish fantasy. Nevertheless, they were disturbed by the fact that the children stubbornly maintained that what they saw was truly a vision of Mary. Their story never changed. Nothing was added nothing was left out.

Eventually, they won converts. People began to flock to the stream to see for themselves. But there was nothing to see. Only the three children were able to see the vision and talk to Mary.

A Miraculous Cure at Sabana Grande

Nora Freise heard about the vision at the spring and wondered if the water would help her. She had been a paraplegic for forty-seven years and had never left her wheelchair in all that time.

She took some of the water. A few days later she was able to stand up. A little later she abandoned her wheelchair permanently. Dona Nora left her comfortable home in Mayaguez and lived humbly with her family near the spring that had changed her life so drastically.

Dora Nora's story inspired others to take water from the stream. Crowds of people poured into the area, some of them even ripping out the roots of the mango trees where the children said they saw the Virgin.

Then it was revealed by the children that the Blessed Mother would perform a miracle on the 25th day of May. The day before, huge throngs began to make their way to the stream. They had to walk because the roads were so bad that cars could not be used. Representatives of the media were there, as well as priests and politicians. People slept on the ground all night. The designated hour for the miracle was 11:00 a.m., and as that hour approached, tension began to build.

It was hot. There was a brilliant sun in the sky and no clouds were visible anywhere. Then at exactly 11:00 a.m. it began to rain! But this was no ordinary rain. The drops were multicolored! Every color of the rainbow was represented in the drops. The Virgin Mary had kept her promise.

The Third Miracle at Sabana Grande

Georgina Palitics lived in Miami and was married to Ismael Rivera Cardenas. She had a chronic neck ailment that had apparently been a delayed reaction from an accident she had when she was three years old. One night she woke up with the sensation that her head was suspended from her body, and after that experience she was not able to hold her head up. Georgina had to be fitted with an orthopedic brace.

The brace was a torture to wear, since it started at her waist, covered her chest and ended at her jaw. She thought of it as being in a cage. The couple went to many specialists and all of them agreed it was too late for Georgina. There wasn't a doctor in the world who could heal her. The disease's degeneration had simply gone too far; Georgina would have to wear the brace for the rest of her life.

Her husband searched desperately for a remedy. The

"cures" that he found were useless. The couple was advised that a change of climate might help, so they decided to go to Puerto Rico. Their arrival coincided with the great furor going on at Sabana Grande. They knew nothing about it, but listened avidly when they were told about Dora Nora's miraculous cure.

Georgina and Ismael decided to try it, too. But getting there was a problem. Georgina couldn't walk that far. They decided to go by car even though the roads were bad. Ismael drove at a snail's pace. There were many obstacles in the road that he had to drive around or move physically before he could continue.

When they arrived at the healing spring Georgina faced another obstacle. There were so many people lined up for a cure that she was overcome by disappointment and fainted.

When she regained consciousness an attending physician suggested that she be taken to the local health center. She didn't want to go there, not yet. She wanted to get to the spring. And her great disappointment again caused her to faint.

At the health center, Georgina slept in the chair that she had brought with her. She had not been able to sleep in a bed since her affliction. Then at 4:00 a.m. she rose and made her way to the elementary school, which was her first stop before reaching the stream. The attending doctor at the school was not pleased to see her. She was in no condition to walk to the stream. She pleaded: "Please do something for me. Take me to the stream. I need to be there."

The doctor nodded. He summoned four National Guard members to go with her.

Georgina said that at the Stream of the Virgin she saw many images, the Sacred Heart of Jesus and many flowers that seemed to float in the air. She heard a voice say in English, "Look forward." She tried to raise her arms but the braces were in the way. She prayed hard. Then she saw what looked like the figure of a nun which stood out in the crowd around her, even at four in the morning. The nun opened her arms and turned in all directions. It was apparent that no one else in the crowd saw the nun. She realized it was the Blessed Mother.

Suddenly, she felt a jolt in her head, which was accompanied by severe pain. She had no explanation for it, but she did feel now that it was no longer important to her whether she was cured. She said later, "The satisfaction of seeing the Virgin was enough."

The three children who had originally seen the vision were there now, but were too far away to communicate with Georgina. The crowd was so thick now that they couldn't get close to her. So they passed the word forward that the Virgin wanted someone to remove Georgina's braces. The woman was already aware of the fact that she could now move her neck. The orthopedic braces were taken off. Georgina held her head high. She was able to turn it. She could walk, too, without help. She had no pain. And as she walked away from the stream, people around her shouted: "She's been cured!"

Georgina returned to Miami and went to the specialists. They could not believe that this was the same woman they had doomed to a lifetime of torture in an uncomfortable brace.

It must be noted that Georgina was not a Catholic. After the miracle cure, however, she converted. Since that day in 1953, she has made it a point to return to the stream every year on May 25th. She has not yet missed a year. Her hope is that some day she will be able to live in Sabana Grande and spend her remaining days close to the spot where she saw the Blessed Mother.

Top photo shows distinct form of Mary hovering in the air over St. Mary's Church of Zeitoun while below the Virgin is said to be holding a baby (Jesus?) in her arms. (Pictures by Mr. Rizk Matta.)

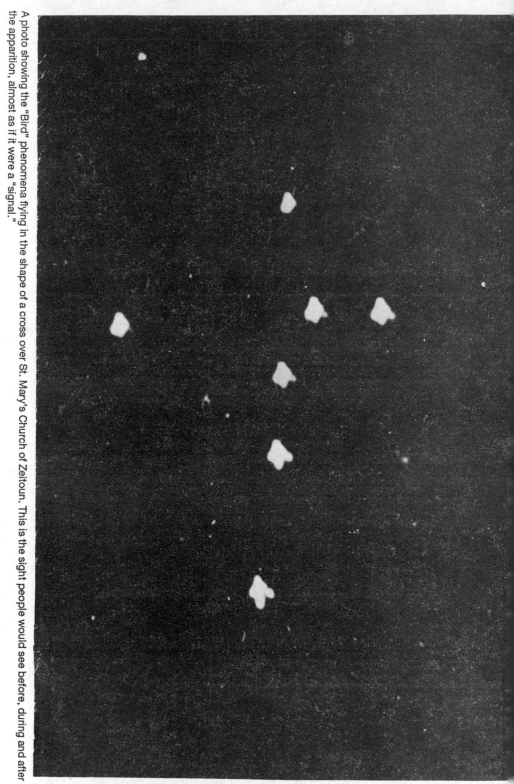

A photo showing the "Bird" phenomena flying in the shape of a cross over St. Mary's Church of Zeitoun. This is the sight people would see before, during and after the apparition, almost as if it were a "signal."

The sorrowful Virgin of Aibonito was seen to shed real tears before a disaster struck the area.

The "Lady in White" of Holy Mountain

Of all the cases of Marian phenomena, the following perhaps best of all suggests a strong UFO tie-in:

Over the years, Peru has seen its share of mystical happenings. Many citizens have reported seeing far distant lights in the sky that behave "improperly," and visionary experiences transpire here as frequently as anywhere else in South America or the rest of the world, for that matter. But there is an area in the state of Huanaco that deserves special attention, for among the strange phenomena reported occurring here includes:

• Mysterious floating lights;

• Unknown flying machines;

• Odd creatures that materialize in the surrounding hills, emitting magical sounding hums,

• And most amazing of all, the appearance of a female figure dressed in white that has become known as the "White Lady of the Andes."

Our first inkling of anything unusual taking place in this particular region occurred when three local inhabitants, or Hill People as we will call them, arrived in Lima after a long exhausting journey from their territory which is located between the central and eastern ranges of the Andes, not far from the edge of the jungle on the banks of the Haullaga, a tributary of the Amazon.

Strange Figure

The state of Huanaco is in itself somewhat of a mystery even to the rest of Peru. Tradition holds that the first inhabitants of the area came from the heavens, and some years back archaeologists uncovered the now famous "Temple of the Crossed Hands," believed to be the oldest archaeological artifact anywhere in the Americas. Made of mud this figure dates back to 4200 years, and studies have shown that the formation of its fingers, wrist and forearm is totally of a different nature from that of the people who now inhabit this region. It is generally believed that a different race must have arrived in Peru in the remote past from another continent. What cannot be explained is the fact that since the statue was made out of mud how it has been able to survive the passing of time and the forces of nature. This would indicate that an unknown ingredient was used in its composition.

An Investigation is Organized

Quickly, the Peruvian Society for Interplanetary Relations organized a fact finding mission to the region. Many interesting stories had long been reaching researchers from this area and we decided it was time to investigate.

The first group was headed by Cesar Vasques Salasi, a scientist from Ecuador. He was accompanied on the journey by two capable researchers, Señor Alessandri and Alvarez. Together they traveled to the scene and interviewed several witnesses. They were even told about a case involving a man who was caught in quick sand and was saved when he was pulled out of the sink hole by two little men with greenish tinted skin.

From all they were told, it was obvious that the majority of reports came from an area known as the Rondo Plain, just north of the city. At an altitude of 7400 feet the investigators set up camp. During the course of that first night strange things started to happen.

Cesar Vasques Salasi later reported back to us that at 9 P.M. all of their group saw two UFOs which were not explainable. A short while later Jorge Aluarez was by himself a short distance from camp when he almost suffered a heart attack. There standing before him in the dark were several beings who were very short in stature, had greenish colored skin and scales on their bodies and tails.

As soon as it could be done, a well-equipped expedition was organized. This time 12 investigators chose to make the long journey which I personally directed.

The first stop was at the home of Señor Fernando Fernandez, who proved to have a wealth of knowledge and was very well versed on UFOs in the region. He said that his research had indicated that most of the strange activity seemed to be centered around the town of Cayran, which is located in a valley and inhabited only by country folk. In Cayran, Señor Fernandes explained, life is devoid of social problems, politics, and crime. The residents live in sort of a communal fashion and are closed to outsiders who interfere in their daily activities.

Residents Draw Back

Upon their arrival in town the researchers were immediately surrounded by many curious people who, when they found why they had come, drew back and refused to answer any of their questions. To them the subject of their trip was "taboo." From what could be gathered, they were upset thinking that the tranquility of the place would be altered. To them, any investigation of the "Lady in White" was a sin, in their eyes at least, very diabolical.

Initially, it looked like they had traveled in vain, that their investigation would not be successful. Luckily, the course of events were changed when two of the team of investigators came across two young boys playing alongside the banks of a stream. The boys were playing with a peculiar looking doll—a wooded figure of a virgin perfectly shaped. This doll fit perfectly the description that has been given of the "Lady in White" Naturally the researchers were curious and asked the boys a lot of questions.

The boys said the name of the Virgin was "La Purisima" (the

"purest of Holiest") and said that she lived in a cave outside of their town. They were not very helpful in giving directions, and would say only that she lived on top of a mountain accompanied by small "angels," and that she called the faithful with the aid of a bell which could be heard throughout the valley.

Said the investigators, "Naturally, we felt as if we were on to something very important, and with the help of a few small gifts, we eventually got the two boys (age 8 and 10) to cooperate.

"After walking over a mile and a half we reached the side of a very steep mountain with two rocks on the summit, one atop the other, at hose base there was an opening that an adult could only enter on their hands and knees.

"For the next two hours we looked for a possible way up to the summit. Being somewhat of a more experienced climber than the rest of our group, I went on ahead, inching my way of the mountain. Slowly but surely, I forged a path by hanging on to outcroppings and clumps of bushes that winded their way to the top.

The Lady Appears

"Suddenly, about half the way up the side of the mountain, I saw a beautiful woman less than two feet tall. She was dressed in a white tunic, just like all the drawings of the virgin. The woman's skin was a strong pink. She had very large, blue eyes and her hair was golden blonde. In one hand she held a red belt, and to me it seemed as if she were capable of reading my mind.

"After a few seconds of indecision on my part, I decided to try and communicate with her. 'Lady, I know you are not a spirit but a representative of another world, whose mission is to do good and look for love between the inhabitants of this planet and yours. I only wish to speak with you, so as to receive your message and share it to those who want to grow spiritually.'

"Before I had finished speaking with the 'Lady,' she started to move away, up the mountainside. To me it did not look as if she were walking as I did not see her feet touch the ground (her tunic was covering her feet). Within minutes she reached the cave at the summit of the mountain and vanished inside.

"Not one to give up so easily in my quest, I tried to follow her. Eventually, I reached the cave at whose entrance there was a small platform about thirty square feet. The platform was covered with flowers and vegetables obviously placed there by the faithful in gratitude for miraculous cures received by the local inhabitants.

"As the others in our party reached the top, I suggested that we search for the bell the 'Lady' used in order to summon the Mountain Folk. I figured that it would have to be rather large in order to be heard throughout the entire valley. Because of its size it would be pretty hard to hide in the cave.

"Taking matters into my own hands, I asked the youngest of the two boys who had led us to the cave to go inside the small opening and see if the 'Lady' was there. A few minutes later he crawled back out on his hands and knees and told us, 'Yes, she is there, but she is not alone—she is accompanied by two angels.'

"Two angels?" we asked wanting a better description.

"Yes, mister," answered the boy. "She is with two little men, dressed in gold."

"Once again I asked the boy to enter the cave and request permission to make contact with the 'Lady in White' and the little men. I told the boy what to say, that we were learned men and wished to tighten bonds with our space brothers. Upon his return the youth stated that the "Lady in White" was willing to come out at midnight. I said that was not practical, since at this altitude we would surely become sick or perhaps even freeze to death. All our geiger counters, telescopes and other measuring devices would do us no good since we didn't have the proper garments to sleep at this high altitude.

"It was obvious that she did not wish a physical contact with members of our group, and so we went away disappointed. But perhaps we shall return some day soon to this region and discover even more about the 'Lady in White' and the "angels" who accompany her in the cave."

126

Miracle of the Weeping Madonnas

From California to Puerto Rico, statues of the Virgin Mary are crying real tears and moving about as if to warn of impending danger.

The mystery surrounding the statue of Our Lady of Fatima which is said to move about and shed tears in Thornton, Calif., a rural community outside of Sacramento, has received its share of national publicity in recent months.

Some months ago an attendant in the church noticed that the statue—which weighs nearly sixty pounds and stands four feet high—had apparently moved down the aisle by itself over night.

Over a period of the next six months—always on the 13th —the statue would somehow find its way to the altar, although it had been in its usual resting place on the 13th of the month, and perhaps this was in some way tied in with the famous apparition. To add fuel to the belief that this occurrence was something in the realm of the supernatural, the statue also began to shed tears. This, many believe, is Mary's way of warning people that some terrible event is going to take place very soon.

Of course, there are the skeptics who point out that church attendance has mushroomed since the story was published in local as well as national publications. Now it is not uncommon for a thousand of the faithful to flock to the church for services, especially around the time of the month when the statue is supposed to move.

By pure coincidence, an *Inner Light* reader, Joyce Davis of Inights Landing, California, also heard of the miracle at about the same time we started work on a new book on the Virgin Mary. This book details several dozen appearances of the Mother of Jesus in recent years and the dire prophecies She has repeatedly given in order to save as many people as possible should there by a global disaster. Apparently Joyce Davis was really emotionally touched by her visit to the church and as PROOF that this statue is no ordinary statue, Joyce came away with a fantastic photograph showing a fiery object which was not present when she took the picture. What she captured with the camera's eye is reproduced in this book (unfortunately in black and white), but let us allow Joyce to tell her own story:

"On the date of December 19, 1982, I walked through the doors of the little Catholic Mission Church of Mater Ecclesiae with heavy heart and troubled countenance.

"I came not seeking signs and proof of what I had heard, but with a prayer, and an urgent hope and desire that I might obtain Divine Intercession in matters that had become very difficult to cope with and burden which had become almost too heavy to bear.

"Being not of the Catholic persuasion, but having respect for all spiritual beliefs that are held sacred in the hearts of devotees the world around, I sought solace in the quiet Sanctuary where pilgrims of all faiths have come of late. I came, because I believe.

"While pondering the wonder of this place, I remembered the words of Jesus: 'Blessed are those who have not seen, and yet believe,' and hope replaced despair; peace replaced anxiety, and I stood there amidst the faithful who comprised a congregation which exhibited various religions, races, languages and economic backgrounds, a fair sampling of the inhabitants of this planetary globe.

"Understanding of Catholic ritual was not my strongest

asset as I sat when I should have been standing, knelt when I should have been seated, and fumbled through the little booklet that had been handed me, unable to determine which page and which paragraph was being cited.

"Music, however, is a universal language, and when the strains of familiar Christmas carols rang forth all present seemed to share a common understanding and seemed to be united in a common bond of Brotherhood.

"Beloved Lady; how I long for the day when this kind of unity will be the prevailing factor upon this planet, replacing the divisions which now persist among the Children of earth. How I long to hear the earth resounding with songs of praise, instead of the constant tumult that presently exists."

"With reverence and humbleness of heart I approached the area in the corner of the little Mission Church where the statue representing the Divine Presence stands, surrounded by Florar offerings of the faithful."

Lovingly did I light a candle, with the hope that the flame which I offered would unite with the many thousands being lit and offered the world around, representing hearts aflame with praise and thanksgiving that we are allowed the privilege of assembling together for the purpose of showing our gratitude for the gift of life, and the opportunity presented to each of us through this Divine gift.

"I listened as the Rosary was recited, appreciating the sacred ritual, but having had very little experience concerning it, other than being familiar with 'Hail Mary.'

"Determined to capture this beautiful experience, lest it be lost in the demands, pressures and chaos that has monopolized my life for the past number of years, I approached the replica statue of the Virgin Mary and preserved that memorable occasion on film.

"After offering my own personal petition and prayer of thanksgiving I, very reluctantly, walked out of the little Mission Church, but with a heart much lighter than when I had entered a short time earlier.

"Upon receiving the processed film, I discovered a very brilliant globe of white light, surrounded by a fiery aura in the upper left side of one of the pictures. Nobody seems to be able to explain to me exactly what this manifestation is."

Though Joyce Davis remains puzzled, there is a possible explanation in that other, similar, manifestations have taken place on a global basis. Later in this book, it is revealed that Mary has repeatedly told of a forthcoming devastating wall of fire which will sweep down over the earth, destroying the chaos that mankind has created out of God's beautiful creation. Known as the "Ball of Redemption," Mary has warned over and over again that God in Heaven is fed up with the conditions down here on earth and will cleanse the planet in the very near future.

In fact, Joyce Davis says that she has now had a chance to meditate on what the manifestation in her picture indicates, "And the answer I have received is: *'For the judgment I AM come.'* A statement which I feel is self-explanatory, and which helps me to remain firm in my conviction that judgement will indeed come upon those who take so lightly the warnings that are being sounded to the uttermost parts of the earth and which are still falling upon deaf ears."

Concludes Joyce, "I pray that the reason for the Virgin's weeping will soon be over, for there ARE those upon this earth who have taken heed of Her urgent warnings, regardless of the taunts and ridicule of those who are presently at risk of being taken by surprise when that inevitable 'Three Days of Darkness' arrives due to their own disregard for useful instruction and the breaking of laws which demand justifiable restitution."

The Sorrowful Virgin of Aibonito

Nothing like this has ever happened in the 160 years since the town, which is at the highest point in Puerto Rico, was founded. According to witnesses, the image of the Virgin Mary has been seen to cry in the local parish, and even the priest who has been taught to be hardnosed and skeptical in such matters, admits that the entire episode has him puzzled.

The Virgin was seen for the first time to weep on May 31, 1983 during a mass at which another, similar, statue was being crowned. The first person to notice the tears was a child who ran and told her mother what she had seen, even though she was not old enough to understand the significance of the event.

Daisy Santiago de Rivera, mother of the child who first witnessed the miracle, tells how the miracle unfolded: "We went to the mass and stayed in the back. Jessica and her older sister and some other little girls went to place some flowers beside the image of the Virgin which was being crowned.

"Then little Jessica asked if she could take some flowers to a second statue of the Virgin Mary and place some flowers around Her. I said she should do this because the second statue looked so sad that she was being left out of the proceedings. My daughter took the flowers, which were white lillies, and placed them by the statue. My sister was there praying. Suddenly, she noticed that there seemed to be tears on the face of the statue. Without saying anything to me, she walked to the front of the altar and waited for the mass to be over. Then on impulse, I went over to the Sorrowful Virgin and I also noticed the tears. I was not able to pray. I thought I must be going mad.

Daisy saw the tear fall down as far as the lips. Her sister, who is a school teacher, saw the tear fall even further. Daisy's husband, Pucho Rivera, a band director says, "Everyone who was there saw it. It was a miracle meant for us all!"

By the end of the service word had spread of the miracle and everyone clustered around the statue of the Madonna to catch a glimpse of the tears. Though there was a lot of emotion, tears and prayers, there was no hysteria. It seemed that most everyone was wondering what message the Sorrowful Virgin was trying to convey.

Teofilo Morales, a devout youth who was assisting at the Church of San Jose that day, explained that many of the faithful went up to the statue and examined the face very closely.

"Many people said that they saw the Virgin crying. I and some other young people climbed over the partition to get a closer look and be certain. I can testify that the face was kind of shiny."

Margarita Gonzalez de Bonilla, president of the restoration committee and resident of the house next to the church also noticed an unusual phenomenon on that day. "I heard the commotion of the people leaving the church. Everyone was scared because they said the statue of the Virgin was crying. I tend to be a bit skeptical so I stayed here in my house. Early the next morning, I went to the church. I began to pray when I noticed, not that She was crying, but that one of the Virgin's eyelids was a little low. I went over to some friends, who were just entering the church, so that they could confirm what I saw. Everyone said it was true. Later, when I went back, I noticed that the eyes were a little more elevated."

The residents of Aibonito don't know what this all means, but they are certain that the Virgin Mary does not cry for no reason at all. They are looking deeply within themselves for answers, as are others who have witnessed the appearance and been affected by the miracles of the Heavenly Mother.

Joyce Davis of Insights Landing, California, took this amazing photo showing a statue of the Virgin surrounded by a fiery ball, similar to the "ball of redemption" spoken of in many of the Marian prophecies which warn of upcoming disasters to strike soon.

During ecstasy girl's body is lifted off ground by unseen power. Below 3 girls witness vision of Virgin Mary.

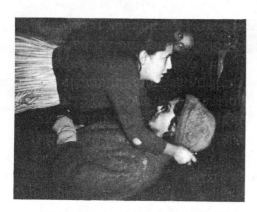

Above: During communion holy wafer appears on Conchita's tongue. Below: She returns religious metal to owner while in trance state.

Visions at Garabandal

Garabandal is a small village in the northern part of Spain. It lies near the Picos de Europa Mountains and is a rugged area, although quite beautiful. The town's full name is San Sebastian of Garabandal and is quite difficult to reach. You have to climb a steep road which begins in Cosio. The population of Garabandal is about 300. There is no doctor in town, and until 1965 there was not even a resident priest. The pastor from Cosio used to come to the quiet town to celebrate Mass every Sunday.

The visions began on June 18, 1961 in the evening. Four girls were playing on the outskirts of the town when they occurred. The girls were Conchita Gonzalez, Maria Dolores Mazon, Jacinta Gonzalez (no relation to Conchita), and Maria Cruz Gonzalez (no relation to the other two). Maria Cruz was eleven. The other three were 12. All were from poor families.

The girls heard what sounded like a thunder clap. When they looked around for the source they saw a bright figure who announced himself as Michael the Archangel.

The girls were awestruck. They said nothing, did nothing. They merely stared at the magnificent figure until it faded from view.

During subsequent days, however, the Archangel Michael appeared to the girls again and again. Finally, he told them that on July 2nd they would see the Holy Virgin.

The news spread quickly, so that on July 2nd Garabandal was crowded with people from all walks of life. At six in the evening the four girls walked to the place where Michael had appeared. In a short time, Our Lady appeared to the girls accompanied by two angels, one of them being Michael the Archangel.

The girls went into ecstasy, their faces radiating the light that they saw around the Holy Mother. The girls described what they saw in this manner:

"She is dressed in a white robe with a blue mantle and a crown of golden stars. Her hands are slender. There is a brown scapular on her right arm, except when she carries the Child Jesus in her arms. Her hair, deep nut-brown is parted in the center. Her face is long, with a fine nose. Her mouth is very pretty with lips a bit thin. She looks like a girl of eighteen. She is rather tall. There is no voice like hers. No woman is just like her, either in the voice or the face or anything else. Our Lady manifested herself as Our Lady of Carmel."

More Apparitions

During 1961 and 1962 Our Lady appeared several times each week. The four girls were not always together during the visions. Often, only one girl would be present. The visions did not always come at the same time of day. Sometimes they were in the afternoons, sometimes in the evening. Often, they were seen early in the morning. The people of the village noticed that although the girls worked as hard as usual, carrying bundles of grass or wood, working in the fields, they never showed signs of fatigue.

The Strange Ecstasies

During the apparitions the four girls went into ecstasies lasting from a few minutes to several hours. Their faces revealed an extraordinary sweetness, beautiful and beautified and transformed as by an interior light. Time did not seem to count; they never showed signs of being tired despite the length of time or their weary uncomfortable posture, kneeling on rocks, with their heads violently thrown backwards, or on cold days of winter with snow under their bare feet and no protection against the cold. At the end of their ecstasy they would return to their normal state, with no signs of excitation or nervousness, but only a deep and profound peace and joy. During the time of ecstasy they seemed to lose sensibility—burns, hits, pricks failed to make them come out of their state of rapture. Powerful beams of light were flashed in their eyes without causing even a flicker. Under normal circumstances these lights would have burned the retina and caused blindness. Their eyes had an open and joyful look. When the vision appeared they fell instantly on their knees, striking the hard rock with a loud noise which was frightening, but they showed no signs of wounds or injuries. They were then unaware of the material things around them, being completely absorbed in ecstasy.

Miracle of the Host

An area above the village of Garabandal is called the Pines. A small cluster of pine trees stand on the hill, and according to the four girls an angel with a golden chalice appeared on the Pines and asked the girls to recite the Confiteor. He then gave them Holy Communion. The incident occurred so often, especially when the priest in Cosio could not make the trip to Garabandal to celebrate Mass.

Films were taken of the event, although it was necessary to use very bright light. The lips and the tongues of the four girls on the film indicate that they were actually receiving the host.

On May 2, 1962 an angel told Conchita that God would perform a miracle so that it would be easier for the people to believe what was happening. He would permit them to see the Sacred Host on her tongue.

By the date of the miracle, July 18, 1962, the town was jammed with people. They came from all over the country. Conchita remained in her home until midnight. She was in a state of ecstasy when she walked into the street. The crowd made room for her. Suddenly, she dropped to her knees and opened her mouth. She put out her tongue. There was nothing on it. Lanterns were drawn near. People stared. Then, slowly, a white host materialized. It was thicker than most and it remained on Conchita's tongue for a few minutes.

Don Alejandro Damians stood three feet away and managed to get the miracle on film. In 79 frames of the moving picture the materialization of the host is quite clear.

Witnesses declare that Conchita's arms were at her sides the entire time. Don Benjamin Gomez said: "The girl's face was beautifully transformed into heavenly ecstasy. Her face was angelic. I can certify that she was there, motionless, moving neither hands nor tongue. In this motionless state she received the Sacred Host. We had enough time to contemplate this marvelous phenomenon without any undue haste, and we were many who saw it."

Mary's Warning at Garabandal

On January 1, 1965 Conchita was told by the Virgin Mary that she would have a message for her on June 18th. Naturally, word spread quickly. When the day came, more than two thousand people were in Garabandal, many of them French, German, English, Italians, Americans and Poles. There were journalists from many countries and TV camera crews from Italy, Spain and France.

Conchita walked form her house at 11:30 p.m. to the Pines. She stopped at a place called Cuadro. Witnesses said she was in rapture for sixteen minutes. The entity who appeared was not the Holy Mother, but the Archangel Michael (Conchita learned later that Mary was so distressed by her message that she could not deliver it herself).

The message which Our Lady has given to the world through the intercession of St. Michael the Archangel. The angel said:

"Since my message of October 18 has not been made known to the world and has not been fulfilled, I tell you that this is my last message. Previously, the cup was being filled.

Now it is overflowing. Many priests are on the road to perdition and with them they are bringing many souls. The Holy Eucharist is being given less importance (honor). We must avoid God's angel with us by our efforts at amendment. If we beg pardon with sincerity of soul, He will forgive us. I, your Mother, through the intercession of St. Michael the Archangel, want to tell you to amend your lives. You are already receiving one of the last warnings. I love you very much and do not want your condemnation. Ask us sincerely and we will give to you. You should make more sacrifices. Think of the Passion of Jesus."

The last apparition appeared to Conchita on November 13th, 1965. Conchita revealed later that she was told that a miracle will take place on a Thursday at 8:30 p.m. Cochita knows what the miracle is, but is not permitted to reveal it until eight days before it takes place.

The Garabandal Miracle

Conchita said: "The Blessed Virgin will not allow me to reveal the nature of the miracle although I already know it. Neither can I reveal the date of it, which I know, until eight days before it is to happen."

No one knows when the miracle will occur. We can't assume anything. All we do know is that the hour of Our Lady is coming. Mary promised Conchita that before the miracle occurs, all mankind will receive a warning from heaven.

The Warning

Conchita does not know the exact date of the warning, but she has been given an inkling of what it will be like.

She said: "The warning will be directly from God and will be visible to the whole world and from any place where anyone happens to be. It will be like the revelation of our sins and will be seen and felt by everyone, believer and nonbeliever alike, irrespective of whatever religion he may belong to. It will be seen and felt in all parts of the world and by every person."

139

October 1917 — The three Seers and some pilgrims after the last Apparition, photographed under the rustic arch erected by the people at place of the Apparitions

THE "SECRET" THIRD PROPHECY REVEALED!

DARE YOU BREAK THIS SEAL?

SEAL OF FATIMA

Lucy's Secret Message

The date was December 1957. Lucy was now a nun of the Discalced Carmelites in the convent of St. Theresa of Jesus in Coimbra, Portugal. At this time, she talked about the unrevealed message, giving additional information. She talked to Reverend Augustin Fuentes, who had been appointed Roman Postulator for the cause of the beatification of Francisco and Jacinta Marto.

When Rev. Fuentes saw Sister Lucy it was the day after Christmas and Lucy was ashen-faced and emaciated. She told the priest: "Father, the Blessed Virgin is very sad because not many respect her Fatima Message, neither the good nor the bad. The good do not because they go along with their way of goodness, of apostolate, of virtue, but without paying attention to this message. The bad do not because the chastisement of God is not immediately hovering over them, because of their sins, and they proceed on their way of evil without paying any attention to the message. But believe me, Father, God is going to chastise the world."

Sister Lucy talked about the secret message, which was to be opened in three years (1960), but insisted that she could not go into detail. "I cannot go into greater detail," she said, "since it is still a secret, one that through the will of the Blessed Virgin may only be known to the Holy Father and the bishop at Fatima.

"Tell them, Father, that the Blessed Virgins and many times to my cousins, Francisco and Jacinta, as well as to me, that many nations would disappear from the face of the earth, and

Russia would be the instrument of the chastisement of heaven for all the world, if before this we did not bring about the conversion of that unhappy nation."

Something to Think About

Sister Lucy's words are frightening. The Blessed Virgin said that "many nations will disappear from the face of the earth." Only one force can accomplish such a catastrophe in the world today, and that is the proliferation of nuclear weapons. If a nuclear war broke out, many nations would vanish and millions of souls with them.

Other words from the Blessed Virgin are also coming true. Russia for decades was spreading its communistic philosophy throughout the world. In Italy, which holds the seat of the Roman Catholic world, there are still between 15 million and 20 million communists. Godless communism was, for a long time, growing in Asia, Africa and Latin America. Sister Lucy told Father Fuentes: "If Russia makes war against the world, she will do everything possible to triumph, but if by chance she is conquered, who knows how many Western nations, before Russia falls, may first be destroyed, no matter how well armed they may be."

The Pope on the Secret Letter of Fatima

Pope John Paul II, on his visit to Germany in the fall of 1980, was asked by pilgrims about the Secret Letter of Fatima. His response appeared in the paper *Stimme Des Glaubens* after his visit. According to the paper the Holy Father said the following: "We shall prepare for trials in the near future. Yes, even if it costs us our lives. Furthermore, it is necessary to give ourselves completely to Christ, and for Christ! The trials can be mitigated by your and our prayers, but to prevent it is no longer possible, because only this way can the real renewal of the Church come about. How often the Church has been renewed in blood! It won't be otherwise now be strong! Be prepared! We should trust ourselves to Christ and His Mother.

Pray often, and say often the rosary. Then, although we will have done a little, we will have done everything."

We published the following excerpt—made by Pope Paul VI for the diplomatic circles—for those responsible Christians who want to be prepared, and who want to lessen the severity of the approaching chastisement. While the Pope's hands are bound in many ways, ours are not, and by publishing the letter we obey only the express desire of Our Heavenly Mother: "Go, my child, and proclaim it!"

The Secret Prophecy of Fatima

"The Blessed Mother's exact words [Lucia stated.] 'Don't worry, dear child, I am the Mother of God speaking to you and begging you to proclaim in my name the following message to the entire world....In doing this, you will meet with great hostility. But be steadfast in the faith and you will overcome this hostility. Listen and remember well what I say to you: Men must become better. They must implore the remission of the sins which they have committed and will continue to commit. You ask me for a miraculous sign so that all may understand the words in which, through you, I address mankind. This miracle you have just seen was the great miracle of the Sun! Everyone has seen it—believers and unbelievers, country and city dwellers, scholars and journalists, laymen and priests. And now, in My name, it is proclaimed!

"A great punishment shall come to all mankind, not as yet today, nor even tomorrow, but in the second half of the twentieth century. What I have already made known at La Salette through the children Melanie and Maximin, I repeat today before you. Mankind had not developed as God expected. Mankind has been sacreligious and has trampled underfoot the gifts which were given it.

"There is no order in anything. Even in the highest positions, it is Satan who governs and decides how affairs are to be conducted. He will even know how to find his way to the highest positions in the Church. He will succeed in sowing confu-

144

sion in the minds of the great scholars who invent arms with which half mankind can be destroyed in a few minutes. He will bring the mighty ones under his thumb and make them manufacture armament in bulk. If mankind does not refrain, I shall be forced to let fall my Son's arm. If those at the top of the world and in the Church do not oppose these facts, it is I who shall do so, and I shall pray God My father to visit his justice on men.

"Then it is that God will punish man, more harshly and more severely than he punished them by the flood, and the great and powerful shall perish thereby as well as the small and weak.

"There will also come a time of the hardest trials for the Church. Cardinals will be against Cardinals, and bishops against bishops. Satan will put himself in their midst. In Rome, also, there will be big changes. What is rotten will fall, and what will fall must not be maintained. The Church will be darkened and the world plunged into confusion.

"The big, big war will happen in the second half of the twentieth century. Then fire and smoke will fall from the sky and the waters of the oceans will be turned to steam—hurling their foam towards the sky, and all that is standing will be overthrown. Millions and more millions of men will lose their lives form one hour to the next, and those who remain living at that moment will envy those who are dead. There will be tribulation wherever the eye can see the misery over all the earth and desolation in all countries.

The time is continually approaching, the abyss is growing wider and there is no end. The good will die with the wicked, the big with the small, the Princes of the Church with their faithful, and the sovereigns of the world with their subjects. Satan's henchmen will then be the only sovereigns on earth.

"This will be a time which neither king nor emperor, cardinal nor bishop is expecting, but it will come, nevertheless, in accordance with My Father's Plan, to punish and avenge. Later, however, when those who survive all things are still alive, God and His glory will once more be invoked and will once more be served as He was not so long ago, when the world had not yet been corrupted. I call on all true imitators of My Son Jesus Christ, all true Christians and latter day Apostles. The time of times is coming and the end of all ends, if mankind is not converted and if this conversion does not come from above, from the directors of the world and the directors of the Church. But woe, woe if this conversion does not come about and if all remains as it is, nay, if all becomes even worse.

"Go, my child, and proclaim it! I shall remain always by your side, to help you."

Sister Lucy Reveals Still More

When you have just read is still not the complete message given to Sister Lucy and her two little friends at Fatima. There was more, and it was revealed when the Rev. Father Agosto Fuertes, Postular General for the beatification of Francisco and Jacinta, visited Sister Lucy. At that time, Sister Lucy was in Coimbra and living as a Discalceate Carmelite nun. Father Fuerrtes said he was received with great sorrow. The nun was thin, much thinner than she had been when younger, and was sad. She told the priest:

"Father, Our Lady is very displeased because no one had heeded her message of 1917. Neither the good nor the bad paid any attention to it. The good ones go their way unconcerned and heeding not the Celestial directives; the bad, pursuing the broad way of perdition, completely ignoring the threatened punishment. Father, please tell everyone what Our Lady had repeatedly told me: 'Many nations are going to disappear from the face of the earth, Godless nations will be picked up by God and His scourge to punish the human race, if we through prayers and the Sacraments, will not bring about their conversion.' Tell them, rather, that the Devil is waging his decisive battle against Our Lady, in that, the fall of religious and priestly souls is the thing that most saddens the Immaculate Heart of Mary and Jesus. The Devil knows too well that when

146

religions and priests betray their high calling, they drag behind them many souls to Hell. We have hardly any time left to stave off the punishment of God. There are at our disposal two very effective means, prayer and sacrifice, but the Devil is doing his utmost to divert our minds from, and take away the taste for prayer. The outcome will be that we will either be saved or doomed."

Lucy's Admonitions

The Carmelite nun had the ability to remember everything that Mother Mary told her during the visions at Fatima. Now, with Father Fuertes, she said: "One thing Father, you must make clear to the people, not to wait or hope for any call to prayer or penance either from the Supreme Pontiff, the Bishops, the Pastors, or the Superior Generals. It is time that each one, on his own initiative, undertake to do works of sanctity, and to reform his life, according to the admonitions of our Blessed Lady. The Devil is striving to get hold of Consecrated souls; is working to corrupt them in order to induce others to final impenitence; is using all the artful tricks even to the extent of suggesting 'updating religious life.'"

We Are Approaching the Last Days

The frail nun continued to talk to Father Fuertes, who did not interrupt the woman because he was awed by her words. She told him: "What comes out of this is sterility of the interior life, and in lay people, unconcern in regard to abstaining from sensual pleasures and total immolation. Remember, Father, these two facts contributed to the sanctification of Jacinta and Francisco: The sadness of Our Lady and the vision of Hell. Our Lady is placed between two fires; on the one hand the stubborn humanity, indifferent to threatened chastisements and on the other, we, whom She sees setting at naught the Sacraments and disregarding the approaching punishment, while remaining unbelieving, sensual, and materialistic. The Holy Mother has expressly said, 'We are approaching the last days.'"

Mary's Three Prophecies

On other occasions Sister Lucy has added: "The Holy Mother has expressly said: 'The Devil is waging a final battle from which we will come out either a winner or a loser.'" Who will win? No one knows. The Holy Mother did not say. This prophecy remains open.

However, She did give Sister Lucy another prophecy, which stated that the final remedies of the world are "The Holy Rosary and devotion to the Immaculate Heart of Mary."

The Holy Mother's third prophecy is already coming true again and again, especially in this day and age. What she said was that She is now offering Herself as a source of salvation, in Person, Her numerous apparitions, Her tears and messages given through seers scattered in various parts of the world.

Mary's Prophecy on the Ball of Redemption

You will remember Mary's pledge earlier that she would appear before seers all over the world to spread her message. She did so on December 31, 1974. The seer was a woman named Veronica, who lives in Bayside, New York.

The Holy Mother told Veronica: "A second nun lies out in your atmosphere: the Ball of Redemption. It is not a myth nor a story; it is a fact. The Ball of Redemption nears!"

What is the Ball of Redemption?

It is truly a second sun, a huge fireball in the outer atmosphere of the earth. This fireball emits charged particles called flares, much like our real sun. These particles spiral around the magnetic field in the magnetotail down toward the North Pole. At times they collide with particles in our atmosphere and emit a light at positions much farther south than those of our Aurora Borealis. In the true Aurora Borealis the particles come from the sun. In the false Borealis the particles are from the fireball's magnetotail.

Mary's Unknown Light Prophecy at Fatima

Now that we are aware of the Ball of Redemption, we know that what Mary told the three children at Fatima really makes sense. She said: "When you see a light lit up by an unknown light, know that this is the great sign God gives you that He is going to punish the world for its crimes by means of war, famine, and persecution of the Church and the Holy Father."

Unknown Light's First Appearance

The time was January 25, 1938. The sky all the way from Norway to Greece glowed like a fiery furnace from 9:00 p.m. to 2:00 a.m. Mary's prophecy came true, because just 45 days later, on March 11, Hitler's troops marched into Austria, and it was the beginning of World War II.

The *New York Times'* London office reported: "The Aurora Borealis, rarely seen in Southern or Western Europe, spread fear in parts of Portugal and lower Austria tonight, while thousands of Britons were brought running into the streets in wonderment. The ruddy glow led many to think the city was ablaze. The Windsor Fire Department was called out thinking that Windsor Castle was afire. The lights were clearly seen in Italy, Spain, and even Gibraltar. The glow, bathing snow-clad mountains in Austria and Switzerland, was a beautiful sight, but firemen turned out to chase non-existent fires. Portuguese villagers rushed in fright from their homes fearing the end of the world."

Unknown Light in 1981

On April 12, 1981, Palm Sunday, an unknown light was seen throughout much of the Midwest from Canada to Mexico and in several of our far-western states. It was called an unusual Aurora Borealis, but was it really that or was it still another warning from Mary?

The light was described as an orange-red glow that lit up the skies. A Missouri resident said, "It got so bright here you could drive your car without using your headlights."

149

Weathermen, astronomers and the general public were not able to agree on the red glow. Official observers were also at odds with one another. The National Weather Service meteorologists in St. Louis, and Dr. Heiser, an astronomer in Tennessee, saw the phenomenon as the Northern Lights. However, Northern lights are rarely seen south of Canada.

A meteorologist in Washington discounted the Northern Lights theory. He was Col. Dave Torshir a staff meteorologist at McChord Air Force Base. He said the lights were not the Aurora Borealis because the Aurora Borealis does not travel from east to west, as these lights did. He also observed that the Borealis is never seen from Mexico.

More than likely it could have been the second sun which Mary spoke about at Fatima. It was the Ball of Redemption. Believers feel that the strange light could indeed be a warning from Heaven of tragic events soon to come upon us.

Upheavals Are Already Upon Us

On December 27, 1975, a psychic had the rare privilege of receiving a message from Jesus, in which He said: "The approach of the Ball of Redemption will bring climactic changes upon mankind."

If you examine our recent weather upheavals you will understand that the Ball of Redemption, which is a magnetotail fireball, is coming closer to the earth as it oscillates in the earth's magnetotail.

Mary's Weather Prophecy

This forecast was made to a seer on May 1, 1978. Mary said: "It has been made known to you that there will be many eruptions of nature resulting in hurricanes, tornadoes, floods, great heat and plagues upon mankind."

All you need do is examine the recent past to know that Mary was right:

Dr. Reid Bryson, director of the University of Wisconsin's Environmental Institute, said: "The evidence is now abundantly clear that the climate of earth is changing and is changing in a direction that is not good."

The *St. Paul Dispatch* reported:

"No nation anywhere in the world...can afford to take lightly the ominous...century weather forecast covering the entire planet and prepared for the CIA...It is a calmly chilling and scholarly meteorological study pointed to such radical changes in the climate as to cause its authors to warn that... the consequences in political and economic upheaval and international violence will be 'almost beyond human comprehension'...It's imperative in human survival that such frustration and fear of war becomes inevitable because of massive starvation and death...Over vast areas of the earth's land mass the signs now accumulating point to these forecasts: There will be destructive droughts where droughts have not been occurring. The climate changes that have taken place during the past five years can, the experts are convinced, bring consequences such as the following: The Soviet Union would lose lush wheat fields of the entire Kazakhstan. China would experience a major famine. Droughts would grip India, resulting in starvation for 150 million people. Canada would lose 50 percent of its productive capacity."

The 1990s Will Confirm Mary's Prophecy

The World Almanac tells us that there are 220 noted volcanoes in the world, and that 174 of them have erupted in the 20th century. In June 1980, Mt. St. Helens exploded and left miles and miles of total devastation in its fallout. Mt. Etna in 1983 also erupted and turned peaceful Italian towns into utter shambles. The *U.S. News and World Report* says: "A 'killer' earthquake is long overdue in the U.S. Scientists estimate that as many as 20,000 deaths and property damage exceeding 29 million dollars could result."

On July 28, 1980, a very rare earthquake centered in northern Kentucky rattled residents in at least 14 states from Michigan to South Carolina and in parts of Canada. Hundreds of buildings in Kentucky sustained damage. The earthquake registered 5.1 on the Richter scale. There was no known record of other earthquakes in that area. Authorities could not determine what caused the earthquake, which was felt in Michigan, Wisconsin, Ohio, West Virginia, Illinois, Indiana, Pennsylvania, Kentucky, Tennessee and North and South Carolina.

We are now into the ninth decade of the 20th Century and we have seen floods and mudslides in California, Utah, Arizona, Colorado and other western states. We have had droughts in Oklahoma and Texas, blizzards in the South. In fact, snow has fallen on areas which have never seen snow before.

Obviously, Mary's prophecy is coming true. Scientists have no answers for the topsy-turvy weather conditions. They may have to concede that the forces of the supernatural are at work on our earth.

Our Lady's Prophecy Not Yet Fulfilled

Oddly enough, in Revelations 6:12–17, we see that in the vision of St. John: "The Sky disappeared like a scroll that is rolled up," and Our Lady said much the same thing in June 1976 when she appeared before a seer. She said: "My children you must pray more and do more penance, for the Warning is coming upon mankind. There will be a tremendous explosion, and the sky will roll back like a scroll. This force will go to the very core of every man, and he will then understand his offense against his God.

"The warning will be of short duration, however; and then many will continue on the road to perdition, so hard have their hearts become.

"At the end of the warning there will be a great miracle, but scientists will later rationalize it. The miracle you seek, my children, will be a great warning to mankind."

For a Catholic
view of the Mary
phenomenon call:
1 800-345-MARY.

Our Lady on the Chastisement: "Skin will dry up and blow off the bones as if it had never been." Taken by John Brennan of Methuen, Mass., Aug. 14, 1973.

Veronica Lueken
Seer of Bayside

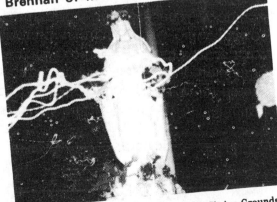

Miraculous photo taken Feb. 10, 1973, on the Shrine Grounds. On the extreme left of picture, in a Rosary bead pattern, can be seen a capital "G" in writing, which stands for God. The coming Warning and the Chastisement of the ball of fire will come directly from God. Notice the letters forming "BY SKY" at the base of the statue on the left. The Warning as explained to Veronica will begin as an explosion in the sky. On the right side of the picture numerous hourglasses are visible, which symbolizes that time is running out, that God will soon pour the cup (chalice) of His fierce wrath upon humanity. All lines with beads represent the many Rosaries being said.

Visions of Veronica

Veronica Lueken lives in Bayside, Queens, New York and is the mother of five children. She is in her early sixties. Her first heavenly visitation occurred in 1968 when St. Theresa appeared to her and gave her poems and sacred writings by dictation. These apparitions were Veronica's first; she had never before been fortunate enough to see such things.

April 7, 1970 was a great turning point for Veronica. That was the day the Virgin Mother appeared to her. Mary told Veronica that she would appear on the grounds of the old St. Robert Bellarmine Church in Bayside on June 18, 1970. She asked that vigils of prayer be held at that site and that full directions be given to the clergy of the parish to prepare for Our Lady's first visit there. Our Lady also requested that a Shrine and a Basilica be erected on her chosen Sacred Site, which would be named "Our Lady of Roses, Mary, Help of Mothers." Mary promised to come on the eve of the great feast days of the church, and those dates would be given to Veronica beforehand. The Blessed Mother also instructed Veronica to disseminate the messages given to her throughout the world.

Our Lady requested that the rosary be recited aloud by the crowd during the vigil. The crowd should kneel in the presence of Jesus. Veronica was to describe what she saw. And everything said would be taped.

Veronica's Description of Mary

"The sky all about us is turning a very beautiful pale blue.

And the blue seems to be disappearing now, and all about the trees there is a white luminous light. It's very beautiful!

"Now, directly over Our Lady's statue, the sky is opening up; it's almost like a cloud-like formation forming back and opening up directly over the statue high in the sky. I can see Our Lady now coming forward. She's a small figure. She's coming from quite a distance. Our lady is floating in. She doesn't walk. There's no way I can explain it. She is carried by the air.

"Oh, Our Lady looks beautiful! She has on a flowing white gown and a blue sash around her waist, a very wide sash. I don't think I've seen the sash that wide on Our Lady in all the time she has ben speaking to me.

"Now Our Lady is holding the rosary in her hand. She doesn't have it about her waist. She's extending the rosary in front of her, and now she's taking the crucifix of the rosary and making the sign of the cross: In the name of the Father, and of the Son, and the Holy Ghost.

Veronica's Prophecies

As we know, the three prophecies at Fatima were the early deaths of Jacinta and Francisco, the Second World War, and the prophecy which is still supposed to be a secret.

Veronica, prophet of Bayside, has been told many things by Mary. We relate some of them here, along with the date of the prophecy and the date on which the prophecy was realized.

On September 13, 1978, our Lady told Veronica: "You must pray now for your new Vicar. There is a foul plan afoot against him."

On September 28, 1978, just 15 days after Veronica's vision, Pope John Paul I died at 11 p.m.

Had a foul plan been afoot against him? We don't know. However, there were suspicions. One publication stated: "The death was so sudden (only 34 days after his election) and unexpected being that the Pope was in good health. Many believed that evidence indicated foul play, and clamors then arose for a complete inquest and autopsy. Circumstances surrounding his sudden passage, such as contradictory reports where the Pope's body was found by his secretary or by a nun after he failed to appear for his early morning Mass, indeed seemed to indicate something being amiss in the Vatican. A front-page cartoon in a far-leftist weekly showed poison being poured into a cup of tea for the Pope."

Newsweek's Report on Veronica (June 2, 1975)

"During services held some 130 days a year, they claim to have seen silver rosaries turned to gold and the spinning of the sun. In December, 1973, when the first group of Canadian pilgrims arrived, hundreds of worshippers reportedly saw the sky open up and the Virgin holding the infant Jesus appear. As evidence, the faithful have a series of Polaroid photos which show strange blurred figures, beams of light and colored aureoles appearing mysteriously at the site."

How Veronica's Visions Are Like Those at Fatima

The need for secrecy was important in Fatima's time and it is now in Veronica's. Mary told Veronica: "There will be a need for secrecy at times, my child, for if you reveal all to the wrong spirits in humans, you will find that it will bring much hardship and suffering to you. Much of the work shall be given in photographs, my child, for your protection and the protection of the mission."

"I have cried. My heart has been torn half in having to witness now what I have earnestly and heartfeltly tried to help mankind avoid. It is only because the Eternal Father feels at this time that a form of warning must be given to mankind in order to save more souls."

Mystery of the Dancing Sun

It would seem that coupled with dire warnings of "doom and gloom," the feminine energies of Mother Mary also offer the strong possibility of peace and salvation for our troubled globe. It is indeed fascinating to note that these visions of the Virgin are strikingly similar to the experiences of those claiming close encounters with angelic-like beings manifesting as extraterrestrials.

Since the late 1940s individuals collectively known as "contactees" have been receiving telepathic messages from the "Space Brothers" regarding possible world-wide destruction due to humankind's maltreatment of one another as well as the planet we live on. There is evidence that both the ecological and the anti-nuke movements had their roots in the messages given by the Space Brothers who actually were responsible for starting decades ago the New Age "tidal wave" that has become ever so popular.

After studying both the UFO and the Marian phenomenon, the similarities become quite apparent. As our Earth is gripped by wars, threats of war, drugs, and a daily assortment of disasters, it would seem that people are looking frantically for spiritual guidance. The Earth energies in a desperate attempt to save itself and those living upon it has arisen to the call the best way it knows how. Millions have turned to Mary as a feminine role model and as a sort of spiritual anecdote to the male symbolism of scientific and military technology. The Space Brothers, in turn, appear most frequently to those who have no strong spiritual beliefs, thus having more of an impact on the collective minds of those who find themselves more likely to be ruled by technology and materialism. The truth is that all the positive energies around us seem to be pulling our world in the same general direction—and it's only a matter of what form the "message" or "vision" takes.

Michael Grosso Ph.D. indicates in his writings for such magazines as *California UFO* and *UFO Universe* that the events at Fatima "seem deliberately, hence consciously, planned. An indication of this was the fact that a 'miracle' was predicted for October 13, three months in advance. Everything looks as if a superior intelligence was using the children to produce a mass effect. The children, it would appear, were selectively manipulated to transmit the overt message while at the same time the manipulator displayed itself in odd ways to the crowd—and at its most spectacular on the appointed day of the 'miracle.'"

The most spectacular miracle at Fatima was, of course, the vision of the spinning or dancing sun. Those who witnessed this phenomena attest to the fact that the sun seemed to leave its normal orbit in the sky and dance about, moving so close to the Earth that it actually dried the rain soaked ground and the clothing of the multitude who were present in 1917.

As late as 1960 author John M. Haffert for his book *Meet The Witnesses* (AMI International Press) interviewed dozens of witnesses to get their first hand accounts. A good portion of their testimony does sound similar to reports of UFO sightings that have been gathered over the last half century.

• "The sky was covered with clouds but suddenly the clouds opened. The sun seemed to be coming down from the sky and looked like a wheel of fireworks, shooting off all colors of the rainbow."—Joseph Frazao

• "It was raining much, and all the people cried out that there would be no miracle because so much time passed and nothing happened. But the little shepherds said: 'Wait, wait a little more.' Then suddenly the rain stopped and a great splendor appeared and the children cried out: 'Look at the sun!' I saw the sun coming down, feeling that it was falling to the ground. At that moment I collapsed, and when I awoke all was over."—Maria Candida da Silva.

• "It was raining. Suddenly, the clouds opened and the sun seemed as though through a window. It began spinning, coming so low that I looked at my watch and believed it was not right as the sun was so low. The sun was spinning and there were clouds of different colors like those of the rainbow. Near me a man fell on his knees and exclaimed, "My God, pardon me."—Joaquim Vicente.

Perhaps the best testimony is given by Father Joao Menitra who had every reason to be skeptical for at the time of the miracle the Catholic Church was very much opposed to the events supposedly taking place at Fatima. He says the following regarding the dancing sun: "I remember thinking that if it rained too much I might have to get under the carriage. It was about noon when a man from Alentejo came up to me and said: 'In about a half an hour!'

"'You know more than I do,' I answered. But about a quarter of an hour later the people nearest the tree were in various colors—yellow, white, blue. At the same time I beheld the sun spinning at great speed and very near me. I at once thought, 'I am going to die!'

"A few moments later, the sun ceased to spin and went back into its place. I looked at the place and saw a truck beside me in which a man in an overcoat stood crying aloud the words of the creed. And I told myself that I was not the only one to be afflicted."

Recently, Vince T. Migliore, a member of the Mutual UFO Network, visited the town of Medjugorje in Yugoslavia where people have reportedly seen the Virgin on a regular basis. The events in this town, located in the hills near the Adriatic coast, have been going on since 1981 and include a mysterious sun-like phenomenon that accompanies the appearance of Mary. "The sun," says Migliore, "appears flat. You can stare at it with no harmful effects. The disk of the sun seems to be silvery or gray, sometimes spinning, sometimes in the shape of a child's toy. Some pilgrims describe the disk of the sun as similar to the form of a communion wafer." Also associated with the visions are strange lights that move about in the sky. "On occasion other lights surround the disk of the flat sun and sometimes circle the central disk or move back and forth toward the church where the apparitions are appearing daily about 6:30 PM. Some observers report circles, wheels and rings, like the Olympic Games' symbols that move slowly towards the church and zip back to the sun just before they touch the tower where the apparition is occurring. Typically, hundreds of people observe such events at the same time. Some also report seeing letters in the sky. The Pilgrims I spoke with reported red block letters that flashed too fast to read. Others claim the letters spell 'MIR' which is Serbo-Croation for Peace."

There is also a "secret" associated with the appearance of the Virgin Mary seen most often in the village by a group of children. Supposedly, when the last "secret" is told to them the apparitions will come to a halt.

We should also take into consideration the factor of the many photos of UFOs that have been taken—both clear and very blurred—in comparison with the multitude of pictures showing the Virgin Mary in all manner of shape and form from the very vague to quite defined. If one wasn't told these pictures were associated with the Marian phenomenon, they could easily be passed off as having been part and parcel of some widespread global UFO flap.

To sum up, the messages of the New Agers, the followers of the Virgin Mary, as well as the UFO believers, is strikingly the same—though the means by which the message is gotten across may take on several different forms. What was told to the three children of Fatima is as important today as in 1917—and it is simply PEACE—LOVE—HARMONY and JUSTICE for all who share our world now and in the future.

Amen.